AF225269

SYDNEY WARBURG

HITLER'S SECRET BACKERS

THE FINANCIAL SOURCES OF NATIONAL SOCIALISM

Sydney Warburg
(1880–1947)

The pen name "Sydney Warburg" represents either an individual author or a collective of anonymous writers. They authored a book detailing the financial backing of the Nazi Party by American bankers from 1929 to 1933. The Dutch title of the book, *"De geldbronnen van het Nationaal-Socialisme: drie gesprekken met Hitler,"* alludes to three conversations that Warburg claimed Sydney would have had with Adolf Hitler. The original attribution of the text is *"Door Sydney Warburg, vertaald door J.G. Schoup"* (By Sydney Warburg, translated by J.G. Schoup).

Published by Omnia Veritas Ltd

www.omnia-veritas.com

© Omnia Veritas Limited - 2015

Publisher's Note

The newspaper clipping that appears below appeared in many major papers throughout the U.S. and was received by all major TV networks. None of the TV networks carried the story to the best of our knowledge.

The last line of the UPI release says the manuscript would be republished Dec. 1 of 1982. On Jan. 4, 1983, we received word that the publisher had "changed his mind" and would not reprint the document. No reason was given. So, in the last 50 years this book has been suppressed twice. What forces caused this remain unknown, but if they are that powerful, we have every reason to believe that we'll be hearing from them at some future date.

This third release of the manuscript while true to the original in verbiage has corrected previously unchanged errors in spelling and punctuation.

History is now the judge of the book's authenticity.

U.S. bankers aided Hitler, book claims

MUNICH, West Germany (UPI) — A publishing firm claimed Friday to have discovered a book that alleges American bankers supplied Adolf Hitler with millions of dollars to help build up his Nazi party.

Droemer Knaur publishers said they received a copy of the book from a Dutch doctor and were convinced that it was authentic.

They said the book, written by the late U.S. banker Sidney Warburg, disappeared during the war.

Warburg, a joint owner of the New York bank Kuhn Loeb and Cie. described in the book three conversations he held with Hitler at the request of American financiers, the Bank of England and oil firms to facilitate payments to the Nazi party, the publisher said.

The book alleged that Hitler received $10 million from Kuhn Loeb and Cie. during 1929, further payments of $15 million in 1931, and $7 million when Hitler took power in 1933, the publishers said.

They said Warburg described himself in the book as the "cowardly instrument" of his American banking colleagues for having arranged deals with Hitler.

The book originally was published in Holland in 1933, shortly before Warburg's death, but disappeared during the war after its translator and publisher were murdered, the publisher's spokesman said.

He said it was thought the Nazis carried out the murders and destroyed copies of the book to avoid being discredited.

The book will be republished Dec. 1st under the title "How Hitler Was Financed," he said.

Introduction

The book you are about to read is one of the most extraordinary historical documents of the 20th century.

Where did Hitler get the funds and the backing to achieve power in 1933 Germany? Did these funds come only from prominent German bankers and industrialists or did funds also come from American bankers and industrialists?

Prominent Nazi Franz von Papen wrote in his MEMOIRS (New York: E. P. Dutton & Co., Inc. 1953) p. 229, "… the most documented account of the National Socialists' sudden acquisition of funds was contained in a book published in Holland in 1933, by the old established Amsterdam publishing house of Van Holkema & Warendorf, called DE GELDBRONNEN VAN HET NATIONAAL SOCIALISME (DRIE GESPREKKEN MET HITLER) under the name 'Sidney Warburg.'"

The book cited by von Papen is the one you are about to read and was indeed published in 1933 in Holland, but remained on the book stalls only a few days. The book was purged. Every copy — except three accidental survivors — was taken out of the bookstores and off the shelves. The book and its story were silenced — almost.

One of the three surviving copies found its way to England, translated into English and deposited in the British Museum. This copy and the translation were later withdrawn from circulation, and are presently "unavailable" for research. The second Dutch language copy was acquired by Chancellor Schussnigg of Austria. Nothing is known of its present whereabouts. The third Dutch survivor found its way to Switzerland and in 1947 was translated into German. This German translation was in turn found some years ago by this editor in the Schweizerischen Sozialarchiv in Zurich, along with an affidavit by the three Dutch-to-German translators and a critique of the book. This editor made copies of the German text and commissioned an English translation. It is this translation that you will read here. Even allowing for the double translation from Dutch to German and German to English, the original lively style is essentially retained. The book is not by any means dull reading.

The original book *FINANCIAL ORIGINS OF NATIONAL SOCIALISM* was branded a forgery. However, since 1933 numerous pre-war German government files have become public information, including the captured German Foreign Ministry files and the Nuremburg Trial documents. These confirm the story at key points.

For example, in the book, Sidney Warburg

claims to have met with an obscure banker von Heydt in 1933. We now know in 1982 from the German records that in 1933 the Dutch Bank voor Handel en Scheepvaart N.V. was a channel of funds for the Nazis. The earlier name for this bank was the von Heydt Bank. Coincidence? How would Sidney Warburg know in 1933?

There are other links. We now know that the German combine of I. G. Farben was a financier of Hitler, and Paul Warburg was a director of American I. G. Farben. Further, Max Warburg was a director of the German I. G. Farben. Max Warburg also signed the document appointing Hjalmar Schaht to the Reichsbank — and Hitler's signature appears alongside that of Max Warburg.

Yet the Warburg family denied any link to Hitler. The Warburgs branded the book a forgery and threatened the publisher unless it was removed from bookstores. In any event, the Warburgs are not accused directly. "Sidney Warburg" was only the courier. In fact, all the bankers named are gentiles, not Jewish.

In 1949 James P. Warburg made a sworn affidavit which compounds the mystery. Warburg denied he had even seen the "Sidney Warburg" book, yet branded it as a complete forgery! Furthermore, careful reading of the James Warburg affidavit shows that his denial refers to another book published by one of the translators, Rene Sonderegger, and not the "Sidney Warburg" book.

And just to deepen the mystery, this Warburg affidavit is published in Fritz von Papen's MEMOIRS—the very same source that recommended Sidney Warburg as a source of accurate information on the financing of Hitler (and Papen was, of course, a prominent Nazi).

Even today a mystery surrounds the document. There is a ring of authenticity about the original explanation for its publication — that an individual member of the Warburg family wanted to warn of the coming European war.

Who's Who in the Book

- "Rockefeller"   John D. Rockefeller II.

- "Carter"   John Ridgley Carter, married Alice Morgan connected to Morgan interests in Paris.

- "Deterding"   Henri Deterding, head of Royal Dutch Shell and strong Hitler supporter.

DOCUMENTATION

Concerning THE FINANCING OF POLITICAL EVENTS

For the Archives of the Schweizerischen Lanclesbibliothek

February 11, 1947

EXPLANATION

The undersigned three witnesses do verify that the accompanying document is none other than a true and literal translation from Dutch into German of the book by Sidney Warburg, a copy of which was constantly at their disposal during the complete process of translation. They testify that they held this original in their hands, and that, to the best of their ability, they read it sentence by sentence translating it into German, comparing then the content of the accompanying translation to the original conscientiously until complete agreement was reached. The original book is titled: De Geldbronnen van het Nationaal-Socialisme, Drie Gesprekken met Hitler, Door Sidney Warburg, vertaald door I. G. Shoup (sic), it has the mark of the publishing house "Vol Hardt En Waeckt" and appeared in the year 1933 in Amsterdam as a brochure consisting of ninety-nine pages of text, put out by Van Holkema & Warendorf's Uitg.-Mij. N.V.

Zurich, Switzerland, February 11, 1947.

Dr. Walter Nelz
born March 4,1909, citizen of Zurich

Wilhelm Peter
born July 28,1906, citizen of Gottingen

Rene Sonderegger
born January 16,1899, citizen of Heiden

Issued in three copies for the undersigned, with an additional two copies, one of which is made available to the Schweizerischen Sozialarchiv in Zurich and the Schweizerischen Landesbibliothek in Bern.

Sidney Warburg:
The Financial Sources of National Socialism.
Three Conversations with Hitler Translated by J. G. Schoup van Holkema & Warendorf, Publishers, Amsterdam, 1933, 99 p.

HOW IT HAPPENED...

Sidney Warburg said very little, as long as the guests were present. He was alone with me now and he began to talk about the Sinclair scandal.

"There are moments when I want to run away from a world of such intrigue, trickery, swindling, and tampering with the stock exchange. Every so often I mention these things to my father as well as to other bankers and brokers. Do you know what I can never understand? How it is possible that people of good and honest character — for which I have ample proof — participate in swindling and fraud, knowing full well that it will affect thousands. The powers in Sinclair Trust have brought in millions of dollars to Wall Street, but ruined thousands of savers. When one questions the reasons for the dishonest and morally indefensible practices of financial leaders one never gets an answer. Although their private lives are orderly and good, it can't be that they discard their true characters as soon as they enter the financial world, forgetting all concepts of honesty and morality in favor of money, sometimes millions of dollars."

The struggle of conscience visible in these words of Sidney Warburg, son of one of the largest bankers in the United States, member of the banking firm Kuhn, Loeb & Co., N.Y., is the tragedy of his life. He was never able to free himself from his connections with that milieu, whose deepest motives he could never completely grasp.

Those words, spoken in 1928, perhaps explain what I asked myself in 1933, why he finally decided to tell the world how National Socialism was financed. In doing so he dutifully did not shove his own role into the background, but confessed his personal participation honestly.

When I received the manuscript from him, along with the request to translate it, I felt that the tragedy in the author's life had reached a final point, forcing him to make the honest confession contained in the following pages. This is my first step towards inner freedom that I wish for him from all my heart, because he has the courage to say in front of the whole world: "They made it possible, but I was their cowardly errand-boy!"

If the "poor world" and "poor humanity" — words with which the author ends his work — do not understand his cry, then his admission was an act of courage, which was necessary to make it. To have this courage means to break with old circles and to expose former friends to the world as men without conscience, especially while revealing one's own full, undisguised participation in the process.

October 1933
The Translator

1929

Money is power. The banker knows how to concentrate and manage it. The international banker carries on international politics. He is obliged to do this by the central government of the country in which he is settled, because the government influences the bank of issue. In other countries this is called the national bank. Whoever understands what was concealed behind the word "national" in the last few years and what is concealed there still, also knows why the international banker cannot keep himself out of international politics.

The American banking world had been developing for months at a brisk tempo. We were experiencing a boom, and we knew it. Pessimists predicted a sudden fall, but every day we wrote out larger orders, and Wall Street itself made fun of the pessimists. Wall Street gave money to the whole world — even the far-away Balkan Peninsula, whose states we had heard named in school and had long forgotten, received credit, their obligations were sold, speculators pounced on them and the rate of exchange rose. Political economists are still not in agreement today, 1933, as to why the pessimists were right about specifically 1929, not a year earlier or later. 1929 was the beginning of a miserable epoch for Wall Street, which has still not ended.

The rate of exchange did not collapse, the usual term for a decline, but simply plummeted, and in a few weeks the credit-mania in New York was completely over. Agents from credit-seeking European states had to go back home empty-handed. America seemed to have no more money. In hard times it is the custom here for men in power not to keep their views silent. The leading newspapers published interviews with Hoover, McCormick, McKenna, Dawes, Young and numerous others, but it didn't help us on Wall Street. We were living in hell.

Whenever one was called to answer the phone, upon one's return, the prices for steel, Anaconda, Bethlehem, and the leading oil companies had fallen by ten to twenty points. The fall in share prices attracted everyone, whether they wanted it or not, and I know many aserious, respectable banker of excellent reputation, who considered speculation on the rates of exchange to be criminal, but then went ahead and participated himself. He would do this openly, without asking his broker to camouflage his orders or keep them secret from the market.

I said already that we were living in hell, Now, 1933, one remembers those days, but no one can picture the actual situation without having lived through it. We can't forget that the whole world looked to Wall Street, and that London, Paris, Amsterdam, Berlin all were involved in the tension

New York lived in. For that reason the crash on Wall Street had international significance.

I leave it to others to uncover the causes of the sudden crash. I only want to describe briefly the state of American finance in 1929. Without a look at it, the following would be largely incomprehensible to my readers.

The Federal Reserve banks had huge sums standing in Germany. Credits in Germany had been frozen since the dissolution of the Darmstadter and National Bank, the crash of Nordwolle, the reorganization of the D-banks (Darmstadter, Deutsche, Dresden, and Dusseldorf), the issue of the Young-Obligations, and the founding of the bank for international payments. The case was the same in Austria after the crisis in the Kreditanstalt. French, Belgian, Rumanian and Italian war debts were still being settled, but various debtor-states began to request alterations in annuities and rates of interest at every opportunity. Years earlier the French war debt had been arranged at very convenient stipulations that proved to be all too favorable for France. In short, the United States had in 1929 claims on foreign governments as well as private persons abroad amounting to 85 billiard[1] dollars. This was in April. The American banking world had never been enthusiastic about Wilson.

---

[1] One billiard = One thousand billions 2 One milliard = One thousand millions

Bankers and financiers viewed his idealism as good enough for the study, but unsuited to the practical, international world of business. For that reason Wall Street had never been very happy about the Treaty of Versailles, which had been constructed along Wilson's guidelines. This treaty had been formally turned down because France was favored in it for no reason. That was the feeling in 1920, in 1929 it had grown into open hostility. Even though the original agreements had been altered in the meantime in numerous ways (Dawes — Young, etc.) the fact still remained that France, according to the American banking world, held the key to the economic recovery of Germany because of its favorable position with regard to reparations, and because of its claim to receive these in gold instead of in goods. As soon as one realizes that the well-being of America as well as Great Britain, even the whole world in fact, depends on this economic recovery, then it is clear why the Americans tried to promote the economic construction of Germany and Middle Europe through credit. But France threw a wrench into their plans, because what— ever America advanced Germany, either directly or through London, or whatever London itself gave directly found its way sooner or later to France in the form of higher reparations. Germany could not export enough to achieve a trading surplus that would cover its reparations to France. Therefore it had to pay its debts from its capital, but this capital had been advanced in the form of large credits from America and England. The situation became intolerable. Germany could not continue its unlimited acceptance of foreign currency, and America and England could not lend unlimited amounts.

America's foreign claims had been, for the most part, frozen in Germany, Austria and Middle Europe because of the previously described difficulties. 85 milliard2 (sic) dollars are no trifle even for a country like America. 50 to 55 milliard dollars of this were, according to definite estimates, frozen and the rest was in no way secure, because one had reason to doubt the good will of the former allies — with the exception of England — regarding the repayment of debts to America.

At this point we must go back a ways into postwar history. Ever since the first days after the signing of the Treaty of Versailles, France regarded its stipulations as permanent and sacred, not because of sentimental considerations but out of comprehensible self-interest. However hard it has been in past years to convince the French governments and French financial experts in speech and in writing that more was demanded of Germany than it could give according to the stipulations of the treaty, this point of view never gained entry into leading circles in Paris. As long as the French are not convinced of this truth, international cooperation is not possible. A world economic conference is being held this year in London. I wouldn't bet a single nickel on its success, if the French government does not substantially change its position. In all the negotiations that have been held since 1920 to change the Treaty of Versailles,

France has constantly guarded against a reduction of the reparations due her. Several reductions were put through in spite of this, but France never asked for more than she could not possibly receive, and even knew how to gain advantages for herself out of reductions. France, then, received, also due to the acceptance of the Young plan, the largest portion of the annuities without any conditions attached, and managed to maintain her resultant superiority over Germany. I do not judge France's behavior. Politicians and financiers in France were subject to the belief that the possibility of a repetition of 1914 should be kept open and that they should try to anticipate the danger; to them a prosperous Germany increased the possibility of such a repetition. (The Germans were always the robber barons in Europe and will always be, just as in the Middle Ages.) Germany, according to French belief, must remain economically weak. But the world needs a prosperous Germany, America more than anyone else. Why? Look for the explanation in works on political economy, in examples of practical, international economy, in fat books on the subject containing much idiocy, all betray a complete lack of insight into reality. Political economists are, first of all, primarily academics. They are familiar with banks, factories, business offices, stockmarkets, but only from the outside. Don't forget that when Wilson was still a professor at Princeton, he was known in America as the best political economist. But I have strayed from the subject. We must remember: France does not want a prosperous Germany out of concern for her own security; America and England, however, need a healthy Germany, otherwise both can't be prosperous. In order to keep Germany down economically, France makes use of her claim to reparations, which everyone set at much too high a price, due to Wilson's lack of common sense and to the excitement of victory from 1918-20, and they became an unbelievable burden on Germany. All German governments stood between the frying pan and the fire: demands from foreign countries (mainly France) on one side, and anger from within on the other. If they fulfilled the foreign demands, then the German people cried treason-reproaches and accusations from the people can ring very loudly — if they resisted, then a French military occupation threatened. The adventure in the Ruhr came about in this way. It proved to be unsuccessful for France and she gave up additional attempts, but found other ways to make advantageous use of her reparations claim. I cannot explain all of French political strategy in this brief presentation. I would only like to add that France knew how to fight stubbornly against every reduction of reparations, or how to accept reductions if they could be replaced with other advantages. As long as France could bring in its demands for reparations, as long as American and English loans to Germany did not suffice to ensure its economic reconstruction, then this reconstruction had to fall to pieces on the requirements of the Treaty of Versailles.

No one will be surprised when the financial world in America looked around for other means to checkmate France on this issue. If the weapon of reparations could be knocked out of her hands, then Germany could put its economy back on a sound financial basis with help from America and England, and open the door to prosperity to the two largest countries in the world. In June, 1929 a meeting took place between the Federal Reserve Banks and the leading independent bankers of the United States. I found out only later what direction this exchange of ideas took. But first I will go into the international world of oil. There is, namely, an international oil world just as there is an international banking world; that must certainly be known to you. Oil kings are voracious men. Standard Oil and Royal Dutch are good friends. Both of these enterprises have divided the world into districts, and each has certain numbers reserved for himself. Each enterprise is complete master of the territory allotted to him. These people have amassed great profits through the years in this way. But Soviet Russia then spoiled everything by introducing strong competition against Standard Oil and Royal Dutch. Since that time the companies make only six to seven percent profit from their capital, but that isn't enough to satisfy the directors' greed. The Russian competition was especially successful in Germany, because various German governments made overtures to the new leaders of Russia, trying through credits, etc. to allow Russian oil and gas easier access to the German market over any other country. Be patient for a few more lines, and you will understand why representatives of Standard Oil and Royal Dutch were present at the conferences held by the Federal Reserve Banks in 1929 with American bankers. I will not expound any longer on international financial affairs, but will relate simply the part I played at the above-mentioned conference in 1929, what the assignment was that resulted for me, and how I carried it out. This confession is dry and boring for devotees of fantastic tales and they will simply throw it away. My narrative is even less suited to those who know that real life writes more thrilling and suspenseful tales than the boldest fantasy a fiction writer can invent, because to them only murder, manslaughter, theft, blackmail, threats, divorce and sex-appeal are suspenseful. My narrative is the faithful description of four conversations I had with the 'rising man' in Europe, Adolf Hitler. I don't intend to write a work of literature because I am only relating my own experiences, everything I heard and learned, and I will insert my own opinions here and there so my readers can better orient themselves. In publishing my experiences I don't mean to awaken hatred against persons, but to expose the misdeeds of a system that controls the world, and that can allow what I myself participated in to happen. "Can allow to happen" is not the right expression. What actually happened is what I mean.

In July, 1929 I was invited to come to the offices of Guaranty Trust in New York the next day, to have a discussion with Carter, the President-Commissioner of the bank. Carter was alone and began without formalities. The next day a meeting was to take place among the directors of Guaranty

Trust, at which the President-Commissioners of the other Federal Reserve Banks, as well as five independent bankers, the young Rockefeller and Glean from Royal Dutch would be present. Carter had spoken to the men about me at the earlier meeting, the one I knew had occurred in June, and they all agreed that I was the man they needed. I speak perfect German and I spent four years working in Hamburg at a banking firm we were friends with. Carter told me what the situation was. I knew all about the international financial problems, he didn't need to say anything on that subject. I knew also how the New York banking world was looking around for the means to end France's misuse of reparations demands. I received a short resume of what France had done in the field of international financial politics. Carter also knew that London felt the same way as New York. I would then be informed as to what would be discussed the following day, but in any case he could depend on my presence at the meeting.

Naturally I came the next day. Carter and Rockefeller dominated the proceedings. The others listened and nodded their heads. The issue of concern was — using Carter's words — very simple. It was clear to every one of us that there was only one way to free Germany from the financial clutches of France, and that was revolution. The revolution could be carried out by two different political groups. The German Communists came into question first, but if a Communist revolution succeeded in Germany, then the power of Soviet

Russia would be strengthened and the Bolshevist danger to the rest of the world would be increased. There remained a revolution activated by German Nationalist groups. There were actually several groups of this persuasion, but no political movement was radical enough to bring about a real overthrow of the state in Germany, if necessary with force. Carter had heard a bank director in Berlin speak about a certain Hitler. Rockefeller himself had read a short essay in a German-American leaflet about the Nationalist movement led by this man Hitler (he said "Heitler"). It had been decided at the earlier meeting to make contact with "this man Hitler" and to try to find out if he were amenable to American financial support. Now the question was clearly addressed to me: would I be prepared to go to Germany, get in touch with him, and take the necessary steps to arrange this financial aid? It must be taken care of quickly, because the sooner the Nationalist group in Germany could be built up the better. It should be emphasized in my negotiations with Hitler that an aggressive foreign policy was expected of him, he should stir up the Revanche-Idee against France. The result would be fear from the French side, and consequently greater willingness to ask for American and English help in international questions involving eventual German aggression. Hitler should naturally not know about the purpose of the assistance. It should be left to his reason and resourcefulness to discover the motives behind the proposal. The next topic of conversation was that I should find out from Hitler how much money he needed to bring about a complete revolution of the German state. As soon as I knew this, then I should report to Carter, in the Guaranty Trust's secret code, which European bank the amount, in my name, should be sent to, so I could then turn it over to Hitler. I accepted the assignment. Why? When I am asked this question I don't know what to answer. In 1929 I would perhaps have said: because I feel the same way as Carter. But when does a man ever know if he is acting for good or evil? Actually that is irrelevant here. I am relating what occurred through my participation.

Three days later I found myself on board the Isle de France with destination Cherbourg; twelve days later I was in Munich. I traveled with a diplomatic pass, with letters of recommendation from Carter, Tommy Walker (not yet compromised at that time), Rockefeller, Glean, and from Hoover. The diplomatic world was as open to me as society, the banking world, and, last but not least, government circles.

Hitler was not easy to reach. The man was either cowardly or feared making himself cheap. The American consul in Munich did not succeed in bringing me in contact with Hitler's Nationalist group. I lost eight days' time thereby. I decided to take matters into my own hands and went to the mayor of Munich, Mayor Deutzberg, with a recommendation from the American consul. The mayor promised us that the next day I would have a report as to when Hitler would receive me, but I doubted his word. He hadn't promised too much, though, because the next day a friendly letter from Deutzberg arrived at the porter of my hotel in the course of the morning, stating the day and hour Hitler would receive me in the beer cellar. I just had to give my name to the waiter in the cafe and I would be brought to Hitler. All this gave me the impression of secret Mafia methods. I went, and everything ran as planned. Behind the huge hall of the beer cellar is a red, old-fashioned room in which Hitler sat between two men at a long table. I have often seen the man in pictures, but even without having seen him in magazines I would have known that Hitler was the middle one. The three men stood up, each introduced himself, the waiter brought me a huge mug of beer and I could begin. Of course, I didn't want to bring up my assignment in the presence of the two companions. I wanted a confidential discussion between us two. Hitler whispered with the two men and said to me in a sharp tone of voice: "This is not my usual custom, but if you show that you have references, I will consider it." I gave him a few introductory letters. He delayed no longer. One look at the two men sufficed to make them disappear.

I then laid all my reference letters on the table and requested Hitler to take note of them. After he had read the letters he asked me if I planned to report my conversation with him in an American newspaper. I answered negatively. That made a visible impression on him. "I don't think much of journalists," said Hitler immediately. "Especially American journalists." I didn't ask why. It didn't interest me. Cautiously I posed several questions to him. I got an evasive answer to each one, instead of a clear yes or no. In between Hitler finished his huge beer mug and rang. Immediately the waiter who had led me in came and took an order. The new mug must have loosened his tongue, because he then took off.

"I find the Americans the most likeable of all foreigners. They were the first to help us after the war. Germany will not forget that. I am speaking of a new Germany. What do you think of our movement over there in your country?.. .Our party platform is translated into English after all. Soon, time will be telling them what we want. The German people are suffering in slavery because of the reparations demanded by the Treaty of Versailles. Freedom no longer exists for Germans, either at home or abroad. Our governments have consisted of cowards and traitors since 1918, each one is corrupt. The people believed the new leadership. Jews and Marxists are the masters here. Everything revolves around money. Discipline and order no longer exist. The German official is untrustworthy. A tragedy for the country... no one thrives under this rabble. Nothing can be expected of the Reichstag and Landtag. All the political parties carry on disgraceful, shady dealings. The government lets foreign countries dictate its laws, instead of showing its teeth and realizing that the German people are still capable of resistance. The people are much better than the governments... How can this be changed? We are carrying on an intensive propaganda campaign against treason and blackmail. We have no more than two daily newspapers and our local organizations are growing continually. They think they are hindering our movement by banning uniforms. Nonsense. The uniform is nothing without the spirit. We will continue to work on the spirit of the people, the discontent must spread, unemployment must pick up, only then can we make headway. The government is afraid, because we have proven that we know the right path to the hearts of the people. We offer work and bread. We can also give it, as soon as an enlightened people realizes it has a right to live and take its place among nations. The Reichswehr[2] has developed everywhere by our own efforts and our divisions, through strict discipline. We are not sitting on a Utopia of Jewish and Marxist bastards. Our platform is German, and we will not give in an inch."

Hitler made a singular impression on me. His short, choppy lines of thought, his chatter, his confused rambling without serious proof made me think that this man was empty inside, and could bring on a wild demagogy with his inflated speech. I mentioned the organization of his movement.

"A strong spirit of solidarity controls our movement. Many of the unemployed from the big

---

[2] German National Army.

cities have joined up, many middle-class people from smaller areas and many farmers from the Platten Lande. Our people give from what little they have to keep our movement going. Dishonesty and betrayal can't occur because I have everything in my own hands. The exemplary training of our people draws all the finances automatically to the central point here in Munich, and I am that central point..."

"Force? But that is taken for granted. A large movement practically can't be developed without force. The stupid chatter of the pacifists is just laughable. Those people aren't living. Life is strength. Life is force. Look at nature, look at the animal world, there the only law is the law of the strongest... towards foreign countries? It may work out no other way. I want to leave America out of consideration, but not other countries. Do you think Germany will get back its colonies without force, or Alsace-Lorraine, or the huge Polish territories, or Danzig?... Money? That is the crucial issue; money can only be earned when the German people are free to establish their economic stability, then we can grab the most favorable opportunity to fight for our rights with the strength of our weapons... France is our enemy, the other earlier allies are our competitors, that is an important distinction... Swindling by Jewish banks must come to an end. Speculators from Galicia are stripping away the income of the middle class. Huge department stores are squeezing out small tradesmen... Taxes and rents should be regulated and done away with ... "Hitler stuck his hand in the opening of his brown shirt. "Here is our platform. You can find everything in there that we have set before us."

It was time for me to bring up the purpose of my visit. He wouldn't let me talk. "Difficulties? Of course there are difficulties, but they don't hinder me. I have made the liberation of the German people my life's goal, and either I will win or be ruined. Our biggest difficulty is that the people have become apathetic after years of neglect. That is why we need a forceful, persuasive propaganda, that stirs up their minds. Propaganda like this costs money… No, we can't demand large dues from our members, I already had to lower them because many couldn't afford them…There is sympathy for our movement in some circles, especially among the nobility. These sympathies are not pure, though, and we are not sure of them. I don't want to be the servant of the monarchists' movement in Germany. All aristocrats here are infected with monarchistic sentiments, and I won't let them into the movement for that reason, without being certain of their conviction. Even then they are under strict control by our leaders…We can't count on sympathy from the large capitalists yet, but they will have to support us when the movement has become powerful. What do people in America think of our movement?"

The American interpretation of his party seemed to interest Hitler particularly. I gave him the same answer as before, that we in America knew too little of his efforts to form an opinion. Again he mentioned the difficulties. "There are many workers who are susceptible to our propaganda, but their own interests keep them from joining the movement. The Social Democratic unions have huge funds at their disposal. In these times it is naturally almost impossible for many to miss paying dues to the unions. We are looking for the means to attract sympathetic elements in the unions into our movement. They can perform a useful service for us by influencing the minds of their colleagues. At the moment I am working on a big plan for our own press office here in Munich, and a publishing office with branches in Berlin, Hamburg, and one city on the Rhine. We haven't worked on Northern Germany yet, and the Rhine provinces are on the way. Bavaria is generally favorably disposed, as well as Saxony."

It became more and more difficult to carry out my assignment. Hitler seemed to like hearing himself talk, and when I tried to put in a small word that could lead to the purpose of my visit, he changed the subject to something else. He continued...

"President Hindenburg is not sympathetic to our movement, but he will certainly not oppose the will of the people when the time comes. The clique of aristocrats surrounding him is afraid of the rising power of the German people, because we can demand that they be taken to account for their weak, cowardly position towards foreign countries and Jewish capitalists," Suddenly he was silent, watched me for a long time, then said acidly: "Are you also a Jew? No, luckily, certainly of German origin. Yes, I can tell from your name." Now I had the opportunity to refer to the difficulties in Hitler's movement, and came out directly with the plan for financial help.

"If that were possible, there would be nothing we couldn't achieve. Our movement will die without arms. They can take the uniforms away from us, but our principles will spread. We do need weapons, though…Making deals doesn't bother me, and I can get weapons everywhere with money. We have set up a school for arms training here in Munich, and it is highly favored by the movement."

At this point I brought up my carefully worded proposal and asked for Hitler's estimate of the amount. This seemed to perplex him. He rang. A whispered conversation with the waiter. Hitler played nervously with his notebook, seemingly deep in thought. A tall, thin man of about forty, looking militaristic in a brown uniform, came in. Hitler offered him a seat next to him. I was not introduced. Without any preface Hitler asked him how much was needed to spread the movement intensively all over Germany.

"We have to take the North and the Rhine areas into account. We must remember that we can accomplish a great deal by helping the unemployed who are still members of unions, and we can't forget how much we need to completely fulfill our plans for Storm-Detachments. Armaments cost a great deal, and smugglers demand high prices." Von Heydt took a long pencil from the table and began to figure on the back of a beer plate. Hitler leaned an arm on his chair and followed his calculations. Then he took the plate from von Heydt and thanked him in a tone of voice signifying clearly that he should leave us alone. "Please remember that for us to make a calculation in our circumstances is not easy. First of all, I would like to know how far your backers are prepared to go, and second, if they will continue supporting us once the initial amount has been spent. Von Heydt has made a calculation here that I fundamentally agree with, but I first want to know what you think of these two points; then another problem is, that we have based our estimate on existing plans when there are still many others under considerations that will be put into effect once the first have been completed. I am thinking of, specifically, the training and education of our detachments in the use of gliders, as well as uniforms for the unemployed — the ban on uniforms is harmless — and of still other plans."

Of course I could not answer him, and I made it clear once again that this first meeting was intended primarily to establish contact. His questions as to the amount of financial help would depend on whether my backers would actually come up with the financial aid, only then could a maximum limit be determined. This didn't seem to please Hitler, or he found it too complicated, because he asked me again anxiously if I personally had any idea of the amount to be given him. I was also unable to answer this one. I expected him to ask now why the Americans were making this offer of financial support, but he asked something quite different. "When could I receive the money?" I had an answer to this question — I guessed that as soon as New York received my telegraphed report they would quickly take steps to send the money to Germany if they could agree on the amount. He interrupted me again. "No, not to Germany, it is too dangerous. I don't trust a single German bank. The money must be deposited in a foreign bank, where I can then have it at my disposal." He looked again at the figures on the plate and said imperiously, as if he were handing down a strict order: "One hundred million marks."

I did not show my amazement at his greed, but promised him to telegraph New York and give him the response of my backers as soon as possible. He wouldn't hear any of this. "As soon as you have the report from America, write to von Heydt, his address is Lutzow-Ufer 18, Berlin. He will contact you with further instructions." Hitler stood up and offered me his hand, which was a clear indication for me to leave.

On my way back to the hotel I figured out that one hundred million marks was about twenty-four million dollars. I doubted that Carter & Co. would be prepared to put that much money into a European political movement. I finally concluded that it was up to them in New York to decide, and sent a brief summary in secret code of the conversation I had with Hitler.

The following evening I went to a meeting of the National Socialist party at the Circus. That morning I had received an invitation to go to it. Hitler would speak there himself, followed by a certain Falkenhayn. I noticed again the emptiness of his reasoning, as I had during our conversation. Never a sign of logic, short, powerful sentences, abrupt and screamed out, political tactics of demagogy, persistent rabble-rousing. I sympathized with the journalists who were there to write reports for their papers. It seemed to me that no report could be made of a speech like that. Hitler didn't speak about the movement, nor about the platform, or of reforms he and his followers expected to carry out. He attacked every government since 1918, the large banks, Communists, Social Democrats, Jews, big department stores. His speech was full of words like traitors, thieves, murderers, unscrupulous men, repressors of the people, those who besmirch the German spirit, etc. He mentioned no facts. He was always vague and general, but… it worked. Later I learned that after this evening about 130 people had become National Socialists. I had the impression that Falkenhayn's speech was being used to calm the audience after Hitler's inflammatory words. Dry and almost incomprehensible, Falkenhayn wanted to prove that Soviet Russia was a danger to the world, that there can be no talk of a union of all Socialists, and that the Hitler movement was the first party to bring about true socialism. His success was moderate.

I didn't hear from Carter until the third day. A

short answer, also in secret code. Ten million dollars were made available. I only had to telegraph which bank in Europe I wanted the money sent to, in my name. Carter & Co. evidently felt the same way I did, that twenty-four million dollars was too much money to throw into the wind. I wrote immediately to von Heydt and the next day received a telephone call from him in Berlin. He arranged a meeting in my hotel.

That same evening von Heydt came to Munich accompanied by an undistinguished looking man, introduced to me under the name Frey. I received the men in my room and informed them that New York was prepared to donate ten million dollars to a European bank, in my name. I would then dispose of it according to Hitler's wishes. The payment and transfer of the money must be regulated carefully. Both acknowledged this without showing any sign of surprise, and added that they could settle nothing without having talked with the "Fuhrer," I didn't understand right away who they meant, but when I continued to say the name Hitler a couple of times the little Frey corrected me quite sharply, saying each time: 'You mean the 'Fuhrer'. I noticed later many times that the name Hitler was never spoken in National Socialists circles; he was always called the "Fuhrer." It made no difference to me. The "Fuhrer" then, if that's what they wanted.

I waited in Munich for a report from von Heydt, and two days later a letter came announcing his visit. He and Frey announced themselves again at my hotel. The following stipulations were set before me: I was to telegraph New York, asking them to make ten million dollars available to me at the Mendelsohn & Co. bank in Amsterdam. I should go to Amsterdam myself and ask this banker to make out ten checks of one million each in the equivalent mark value to ten German cities. I would then endorse the checks, signing them over to ten different names that von Heydt, who would also be traveling with me to Amsterdam, would provide for me there. I could then return to America from Holland. I had the feeling they were dictating such a mode of procedure to me because they wanted me to disappear from Germany as quickly as possible. I raised no objection to these conditions and everything went as von Heydt had arranged.

I ran into two unusual occurrences in Amsterdam. At the offices of Mendelsohn & Co. I was received with unusual politeness after I had asked for an appointment with the director, and von Heydt, who stood next to me at the counter, was treated by both lower and higher officials as if he were the bank's best customer. When the transaction had been taken care of and he had the ten checks in his briefcase, he asked me to come with him to the German consulate. There we were also received with a deference and obedience that proved von Heydt's strong influence. From Southampton I took the Olympia back to New York. I went to the offices of Guaranty Trust to give Carter a report right away. He asked me if I would wait and return in two days to give my full report at a plenary session. The same men were present as in July, but this time an English representative was there sitting next to Glean from Royal Dutch, a man named Angell, one of the heads of the Asiatic Petroleum Co.

Carter was of the opinion that Hitler was the man to take risks. They all thought that twenty-four million dollars was significant, but I had the impression that they trusted Hitler's determination and certainty because of the size of the amount. Rockefeller showed unusual interest in Hitler's statements about the Communists, and as I quoted a few lines from the speech I had heard in Munich, he said he was not surprised that Hitler has asked for twenty-four million. I was asked if I had learned how Hitler had intended to arm the National Socialists, and if he preferred to work through parliamentary channels or on the streets. I could only answer vaguely, but my personal opinion was that Hitler, trusting in his own leadership, would take anything he could, and that he regarded it his life's work, either winning or failing completely. Carter asked me further about Hitler's position in relation to the monarchy, if Hitler was ultimately committed to placing the Kaiser back on the throne. I answered by quoting Hitler.

I do not know if further sums of money from America were turned over to Hitler in 1929 and 1930; if they were, then another middleman had been hired.

It is a fact that a few weeks after my return from

Europe the Hearst newspapers showed unusual interest in the new German party. Even the New York Times, Chicago Tribune, Sunday Times, etc. carried regular short reports of Hitler's speeches. Hardly any interest had been shown earlier in German's domestic politics, but now the platform of the Hitler movement was often discussed in long articles with amazement. In December, 1929along study of the German National Socialist movement appeared in a monthly publication of Harvard University, in which Hitler was glorified as the saviour of Germany and given the title of a "rising name in Europe" for the first time.

1931

I have sworn not to expound any longer on international financial relations. This oath was too hasty. I must bring up several more incidents that took place on the stockmarkets of London and New York, in order to give a clearer picture of that which follows. It is not romantic, dear reader, but complain to those who make history, not to me.

In September, 1931 the Bank of England gave up the gold standard. This means a great deal for a country whose financial world considers gold the basis of its economy and consequently practices the gold theory. Since the days of the great Kent, England has used gold as the criterion of its financial system except for a short interruption for 1915–1921. This change of principle and practice in England had great consequences in America. The value of the enormous gold deposits in the Federal Reserve Banks was considerably reduced. But that was not the worst result felt on the New York stockmarket. America was much more afraid of endangering the dollar. It was feared that the dollar would follow the same path as the pound sterling. The American financial world knew that the decline of the pound sterling was the result of French tactics, intended to weaken London financially, preventing further assistance to Germany. The position of New York in 1931 was not much different from that of London in 1929 and 1930, for that reason America was afraid of being left unprotected by the same French tactics in case London cooperated with France. French financiers have proven since 1926 that they are clever manipulators. Poincare is the greatest financial genius of these times. Earlier, American and English financiers and experts had looked down on their French colleagues with confident contempt. The years 1926 and 1931 plus the time in between have taught us that we could learn a good deal from the French financial world. Perhaps I will give some evidence later for any doubtful readers. This is not, however, within the frame of reference of this book. New York was tense.

This tension had turned to uneasiness — the same had happened in London a few years earlier — enormous shipments of gold were made from New York to Europe, and it seemed as if these shipments were destined for the most part for France. This is not absolutely certain. In the beginning we were glad to see these gold shipments, because we had long since given up the belief in the financial legend that huge gold supplies mean actual well-being for a country. But the French people still believed this. When, at the end of September, 1931 and the beginning of October, 1931, between 650 and 700 million dollars in gold had been shipped to Europe in three weeks, we became rather anxious. We are concerned here with so-called particuliers, partial shipments. The gold deposits of the French government still sat in the Federal Reserve Banks. They were estimated at 800 million dollars at the end of October. If this amount was asked for, what then? Naturally we were prepared to pay it, but it would have caused a panic in the States, and the flight from the dollar would become fact. France therefore had the key to the dollar situation in its hands.

Let us go back a few weeks. Hoover had granted an interview to an editor of the Chicago Tribunes, that time. Unconsciously Hoover and the editor played into France's hands. Very few leaders possess international financial insight. Do you know that a Rockefeller, a Wanamaker, a Harding, son of the late President, and I will calmly say, even Hoover, are all childishly inept and naive in this field? I also know statesmen in European countries who know equally little about international finance and economy. It is not a specifically American occurrence.

Let us go further. Hoover told the editor of his intention to make radical proposals very soon regarding reparations to Germany and the regulation of war debts between all states. One could see from the editor's information that it was possible for Hoover to propose the annulment of reparations payments. Most people in America were astounded by the proposal. But France was on the qui-vive. I don't know if in October, 1931 Hoover, on his own initiative, asked Laval to come to Washington, or if

Laval invited himself. In financial circles on Wall Street they believed the latter. So Laval was coming to Washington, but unexpectedly two French financiers came to New York, landing on October 15, the same day Laval arrived. The French financiers were Farnier, Governor-Delegate of the Bank of France, and Lacour-Gayet, former financial attaché to the French embassy in Washington. They contacted the heads of the Federal Reserve Banks immediately, who then pulled in two representatives of the Treasury Department. Many rumors were circulated as to what was being discussed at this meeting. I know from Carter what was generally brought up. He never would disclose much detail. I gathered from this that the negotiations were not always friendly. The French had come to New York to decide along with the Federal Reserve Banks what could be done in New York. They supposed that the French government had lost several million by the decline of the pound sterling and London's renunciation of the gold standard. The weak position of the dollar had caused unrest in Paris, and they wanted to be sure they would not suffer further losses from the dollar. They wanted to know what was being done to support the dollar. Of course, the enormous gold shipments to Europe were mentioned, as well as the huge French deposit in the Federal Reserve Banks. The French were prepared to transfer the sum of 200 million dollars, a sum by French calculation still deposited in private American banks, to the Federal Reserve Banks, strengthening its position. The French, however, added conditions:

1.   The Federal Reserve Banks must guarantee a minimum rate of exchange on the dollar, applying to French accounts in the USA;

2.   The rate of interest for these sums should be raised 4.5%;

3.   A minimum sum should be determined, that France would leave in the States.

Since the Americans were not immediately prepared to agree to these conditions, the French revealed nonchalantly that even though the agreement they, Lacour-Gayet and Farnier, would make with the Federal Reserve Banks was of great importance, it was only part of a general agreement Laval would be settling a few days later in Washington. They had let the cat out of the bag. It was clear that Laval had to dissuade Hoover from his plans for reparations payments and regulation of debts, and that Laval had to make use of the government funds deposited in the S.A. to force the President to give up his plans. No one can say what the result of these negotiations was in New York as well as Washington. The banking world in New York stubbornly resisted the idea of the States selling themselves to French interests on international territory for the sum of 800 million dollars — the French funds in America. It is a fact, however, that Hoover promised Laval not to undertake anything pertaining to the question of reconstruction and regulation of debts without first consulting the French government. When Wall Street found out about this, Hoover lost the respect of this circle at one blow. Even the subsequent elections were affected — many believe that Hoover's failure to get reelected can be traced back to the issue. One forgets that Hoover was in the middle of a difficult situation. On one side, the American banking world with the Federal Reserve Banks at the head, who represented the opinion that Am Erica could readily dispense with the French deposit if it was misused by France to hold moral influence over the U.S. government in the field of international politics. On the other side stood the Treasury Department, whose leaders would do anything to avoid a dollar panic, pointing to the English precedent.

In October, 1931 the situation was tense on Wall Street and the atmosphere was ominous. At the end of the month I received the following letter from Hitler in Berlin:

Our movement is growing rapidly all over Germany, putting large demands on our financial organization. I have used the money you procured for me to build up the party and realize now that I will have to leave the country in a foreseeable amount of time if new revenue is not supplied. I do not have access to huge government financial sources, as do our enemies the Communists and Social Democrats, but am dependent completely on parry contributions. There is nothing left of the amount I received. Next month I must begin the last great action that will bring us power in Germany.

A great deal of money is needed. I ask you to

report immediately how much I can count on from you.

Two things struck me from this letter. It was the first time Hitler had used the word party with me. His tone in the letter was more one of command than one of a petitioner. Although the letter was dated from Berlin, it arrived in an envelope postmarked in New York with an American stamp. Hitler must already have had supporters in the States, specifically in New York.

The next day I was at Carter's, and I gave him the letter. Carter was the leader of the opposition to the 'Old-Wives' behavior of the government, as he called it, regarding the French demands. The report of Hoover's reversal had angered him so, that he vented his fury over France to whoever would listen. Carter was a hot— tempered man. He read Hitler's letter and began to laugh, then swore and called himself an idiot. He said to me: "We are such dopes. Since 1929 we haven't thought of 'this man' Hitler. All this time we had the means right in our hands to put France down, and we didn't use them. Just wait, we will hold a meeting here this afternoon, and I will try to reach Montagu Norman from the Bank of England, who is here in New York. If he comes, then we can play our trumps. You must come too, of course."

The meeting at the offices of Guaranty Trust Co. was fully attended. I can only explain this by the fact that the tense situation of the New York stockmarket required the presence of its leaders, and Carter had reached them all easily. Opinions were divided. Rockefeller, Carter, and McBean were the Hitlerians, if I may call them that, and the others vacillated. First, Montagu Norman had to be informed of the events in 1929. He found the sum of ten million dollars to finance a political movement very high, an opinion not understood by the rest, since it was well known that political parties in England spend huge sums on propaganda. Glean from Royal Dutch shared Montagu Norman's view. He added that there was little aggression against France in the publications of the Hitler movement. He felt that Hitler was a loudmouth and would never act. He also noticed how Hitler had obviously changed his "movement" to a "party," a transformation that would place great importance on his parliamentary efforts. Glean closed his commentary by saying that there had been enough talk, in Germany more than elsewhere, and a man like Hitler would play along with the majority of his followers in the Reichstag without changing anything in the existing situation. Carter and Rockefeller argued against this view, saying that even if Hitler achieved a majority in parliament he could not be dissuaded from the platform binding him to the German people, and was obligated to use what he had written and spoken of as the only method of pulling the country out of difficult times. He would have to go out on the streets with his followers while keeping up parliamentary efforts at the same time, if he didn't want to lose his immense support. It was finally agreed that in principle Hitler should be assisted further, but someone should be directly informed of the situation in Germany and in the Hitler party before the amount was determined.

I was asked if I was prepared to take on this assignment and to telegraph the amount to Carter as before, then signing it over to Europe in the same way as in 1929, or whatever way I thought best.

I was not able to free myself immediately from my own affairs, so after ten days I traveled to Europe.

Much had changed in Germany since 1929. The National Socialist movement, whose "Fuhrer" had received me in a beer cellar in 1929, had reached the upper levels of society and had his headquarters in the same city, in one of the most beautiful buildings in the best part of town. The National Socialists had their own houses everywhere, in the cities of Berlin, Hamburg, Frankfurt, Dusseldorf, Koln, two uniformed watchmen always stood in front of each, day and night as in front of a barracks.

I saw numerous passersby salute the watchmen with an arm movement similar to the fascist greeting, each shouting simultaneously "Heil Hitler." It didn't take much study to see that Hitler's following had increased enormously since 1929. I could cut my trip through Germany short, because I saw the same picture everywhere. On Saturday afternoons and Sundays the majority of the young people in most cities donned their uniforms and marched in formations differing little from military groups. It is true that there were differences between uniforms, but most were brown and black. Swastikas were everywhere, the emblem of the Hitler party. Even women had swastikas on the rims of their purses — the saleslady in the cigar store in Berlin, where I shopped regularly, wore a huge swastika on a thin necklace. This was no silly decoration, the intent to display conviction was obvious. I had a talk with a bank director in Hamburg whom I had known well in the past. He was quite taken in by Hitler and confessed that earlier he had trusted the German Nationalist Party more, but now he doubted their success because monarchists were in control of it, and the German people had not forgotten the treason of the imperial family in 1918. It was hard for me to take his opinion seriously, because he was a Jew. I needed an explanation, so I asked him how it was possible for him, as a Jew, to be sympathetic to Hitler's party. He laughed. "Hitler is a strong man, and that is what Germany needs. The compromises and vacillations must finally come to an end. The German people are not mature enough for democracy. When the Kaiser ruled the country badly, and he alone was responsible for the administration, not one person objected, everyone fulfilled his tasks, understood his duty. The Germans are quite another story from the English and Americans. They must have someone they can look up to, then they will do whatever is ordered just because the strong man is giving the orders. They have always had basically nothing but contempt for an Ebert, even the Social

Democrats, and regarding Hindenburg, they respect him, but regret that he can't act as regent in the true sense of the word. Since 1918 we have had Chancellors who were commoners, who had reached the top of the ladder through politics. No one respected them. A prince of pure blood in opposition to the Kaiser would have made a good Chancellor." I remarked that Hitler also came from low origins.

"Of course, but that is a different story. Hitler worked himself up and did not crawl into a political party to reach his goals, but created his own party from scratch. You will see that Hitler is on the rise. It will only last another year, then he will be the man. He began in the trenches and will finish as dictator." Again I posed my question of how my informant, as a Jew, could be a member of the Hitler party. He passed over the question with a sweep of his hand. "By Jews Hitler means Galician Jews, who polluted Germany after the war. He recognizes Jews of pure German origin as equal to other Germans, and when the time comes he will not bother us in any way. Also you must not forget that Jews control both the Social Democratic Party and the Communist Party. He will have to win these over, not because they are Jews, but because they are Communists or Social Democrats." I interjected again that Hitler was still against Jewish bank capital, I can even say against banking in general. My informant thought I was very naive. He added that Hitler's platform could not be fulfilled on every point, and Hitler knew that very well. "He has to make unrealizable demands to win over the masses, and this is certainly the least that should worry us. When Hitler comes to power he won't have to be so careful of the masses; then he will be strong enough to push through whatever he wants."

Two days later I spoke to an industrial magnate. He was also a follower of National Socialism. I also read all the newspapers, and tried to make a coherent summary of the political streams in the German press; I concluded that the National Socialist Party showed the greatest activity, had established its roots in all levels of the population, and that opposition from Communists, Social Democrats and other parties was lukewarm and definitely uncoordinated.

I became more and more convinced that Hitler was not experimenting, but wanted to achieve a clearly defined goal, supported by the majority of the German people. It was now time for me to contact Hitler and I wrote to the Berlin address I had received from him, and took a room in the Hotel Adlon. The next day I was called to the telephone while I was reading newspapers in the hotel lobby. A voice, very likely a woman's, asked me if I would be in my hotel evenings, and referred to a letter I had directed to the "Fuhrer."

I received von Heydt and a newcomer in my room. He was introduced to me as Luetgebrunn. After a short statement from von Heydt, Luetgebrunn began to speak. It was as if he was making a prepared speech, he glanced at a bundle of notes from time to time.

"Our activities with the unemployed have succeeded against all expectation, but do cost a lot of money. Our organization is military and therefore also not cheap. Our houses in various cities are all set up like barracks, our people sleep there, cat there, everything at the cost of the party. We provide uniforms, those who have the money buy them, but the unemployed should not be driven away by the costs of equipment. For that reason we are obligated to donate free uniforms and other equipment to our unemployed members. Some of our transportation vehicles belong to party members, but we have had to provide our own trucks and other transportation in the areas in which we have not much following. There are party members who are not able to lend us their trucks because they are afraid of losing customers. Then there are weapons to think of. We have to buy our weapons from smugglers, and their demands are high. We have our buying posts on the borders of Austria, Holland and Belgium, but often the weapons are confiscated by the authorities, thousands are lost and we have to start over again. We have not established direct contact with weapons factories; the only one we have contact with is the F. N. Fabrik in Belgium, but the amount we have been guaranteed is too small. Our Storm-Detachments are incompletely equipped. We can't buy machine guns. Revolvers and carbines are not sufficient on the streets, streams of unemployed join up in the cities and every new man costs money."

Luetgebrunn continued in this vein for quite a while. Then it was von Heydt's turn, and he informed me that the "Fuhrer" would receive me the next day at eleven in the morning in his house on 28 Fasanenstrasse. I would just have to give my name to the maid. No. 28 Fasanenstrasse is an ordinary family house. I could not tell from the outside that the "Fuhrer" lived here, no brown uniforms, or any other sign. An ordinary visit to an ordinary citizen. Hitler had aged in the two years I had not seen him. Yet I found him less nervous, more dignified, more carefully dressed, I could say he was more self-confident. He seemed pleased to see me again, because he asked me with interest about all sorts of details concerning myself. Then, according to his usual custom, he began with the main issue without introduction.

"I don't have much time. Luetgebrunn has informed you of everything already. What has America been saying? Give us one more year and we will have the power in our hands. Do you read the Reichstag reports? What do you think of our showing? When one of our delegates stands up, everyone listens, and the red hordes tremble and quiver. We'll get those greenhorns. They have betrayed and sold out the German people, and we will punish them for it. We have prepared a mobilization plan that will run as smoothly as a clock. One of my best partners is Goring. I have entrusted this to him. Our troops can be mobilized over the whole country in two hours to go out on the streets. First come the Storm-Detachments, whose task it is to occupy the buildings, take the political leaders and members of the government who don't collaborate with us prisoner. Then come our other people, who will occupy the buildings continuously, and our organization will be complete. If blood has to flow, then it will. Revolution is not made with a handkerchief; whether the handkerchief is red or white has nothing to do with it. Traitors can only be taught how to behave with force."

I wanted to ask here what the foreign policy would be. Hitler stood up and strode with large steps across the room. "Foreign countries will be divided into two camps. Our enemies and our competitors. Our enemies are first of all France, Poland and Russia, our competitors are England, America, Spain, Scandinavia and Holland. We have no score to settle with any of the other countries. The population of the Alsace-Lorraine must be brought to revolution, as well as Silesia. That is our first task, as soon as we can get power. If France wants war, then war it will be. We don't recognize the Treaty of Versailles. I want to see Germany and the German people free. If we are not allowed to arm ourselves, then we will do it secretly. All German governments have shown all their cards to France. We won't do this. Our divisions are not regiments, our weapons are not war materials. In two years I will build a German army strong enough to surround France. I will have the chemical industry adapted for war purposes. The situation with our competitors is even simpler. They can't live and work without Germany. I will make demands. Wherever German products are turned down by high import taxes, unlimited production must still be kept up. The German people must be totally self-sufficient, and if it doesn't work with France alone, then I will bring in Russia. The Soviets can't miss our industrial products yet. We will give credit, and if I am not able to deflate France myself, then the Soviets will help me."

I must make a small remark here. When I returned to my hotel I wrote this conversation down word for word. My notes are in front of me, and I am not responsible for their incoherence or incomprehensibility. If you think his views on foreign policy are illogical, it is his fault, not mine. I will continue.

"Stalin has made plans, and he will succeed because he has won over the Russian people. I will also make plans and hold myself strictly to them; what the Russians can do we can do twice as quickly, twice as intensively. After one year of my government there will be no more unemployment in Germany. Jews will be excluded, as well as Communists and Social Democrats; the camps I will lock them up in are already being planned. The Reichswehr is already in our hands to the last man. The government hasn't even noticed this, but I will leave them to their blindness — I am certain of my control. Goring and Gobbels, Streicher and von Heydt have been to Rome many times and have spoken to Mussolini, Rossi, Dumini, and other fascist leaders about the whole organization there. We are also building up our organization according to our own circumstances. Mussolini and Stalin, the first more than the second, are the only leaders for whom I have any respect. All others are a bunch of old wives. Stalin is a Jew, that is a shame. Did von Heydt tell you how much we need? When your letter came we calculated everything exactly. Have you any idea in America of how many difficulties we have here? If everything followed the usual political channels it would be easy, but there is not one city in Germany where I am not joyfully received. I will certainly achieve a political majority, but the people must be afraid, in case the NSDAP doesn't shrink from using other methods to reach my goals, in case my parliamentary political moves don't succeed. We can only create fear by displaying power. This is only possible with uniforms and weapons. If a couple of Communists should be killed by a group of Brownshirts, that is of the same propagandistic value for the party as a speech of mine. Mussolini has introduced a new period in politics. He is the first one to carry out domestic policy with something other than big words and parliamentary motions. In short, everything we need to display our party as a power to foreign countries and to overawe the people costs money. I wrote you at that time because our time is running short and the moment has arrived to take the situation quickly in hand. In some places we have been obliged to turn away the unemployed. That is regrettable at this point, because everything can be done with the unemployed if we can only give them uniforms and food. Are you familiar with our barracks? I will let you see one of our houses here in Berlin. I don't need anything from wealthier people who fear for their possessions when things get rough. We need the ordinary worker, the proletariat, they, after all, have nothing to lose. Have you also spoken to Luetgebrunn? He is a lawyer, but an intellectual of the good sort. Generally I don't think much of intellectuals. They always bring up science and historic teachings. What have they accomplished with all their knowledge? Nothing. Now it's our turn, now let the fist and sword speak. Work and fight, surely that must be the complete life. Dreams and speeches have never accomplished anything. Do you also have connections with the Reichsbank? There is supposed to be great confusion there. Once I get there I will clean everything up. Schacht seems to me to be the best of the lot, but he is a doctor, and that I don't like. These people have mostly become untrustworthy because of all their fabrications. We must put an end to this studying and dreaming. Young people must work the land and be drilled so they can fight, if it should soon become necessary."

His pacing back and forth in the room was making me nervous. It could also be that his sharp words and the lack of a consistent train of thought in his conversation were making me tired. But Hitler continued, "If I lived in America, then I would have nothing to do with politics; there the people are really free, and it is a privilege to be an American. It has become a disgrace to be a German in the last few years. We will see that it becomes an honor again. Do you know that they won't give me this shameful name? I was born in Austria, so I am not a German. Ridiculous. They will recognize me on their knees, not as one of them, but as one above them. The Communists are beginning to be afraid, the Jews think it won't really go on like this, and the Social Democrats still believe they can save their skins with parliamentary speeches and motions. The best people here in Berlin are Communists, their leaders complain to Moscow of their bad straits and demand help. But they don't realize that Moscow can't help. They have to help themselves, but are too cowardly for that. The most difficult issue now is our relationship with the churches. The Lutheran-German church is giving me trouble, the other Protestant churches will soon adapt themselves. But the Catholics. You must know that I am Catholic. The Center Party[3] is very strong and can accomplish something with the support of Bavarian parties. We must neutralize this party so that we are the strongest. I know well that there are also scoundrels in it, but I will leave them alone for the time being. The Bishops are coming forward against National Socialists in some districts, there are priests who give no absolution to National Socialists and deny them communion. A good beating would change this, but that is not good tactics right now; we have to wait."

"So von Heydt mentioned no sum, nor did Luetgebrunn. No, he couldn't, he didn't know the amount. You will see, we have calculated

---

[3] Catholic Party

everything exactly, and will leave the choice up to your backers. There are two possibilities. Either we go out on the streets as soon as our Storm-Detachments are completely organized, which will take three months after we get the money. Or we work persistently with votes and keep our troops in readiness if they should be needed. The first we call the revolution plan, the second we call the "legal takeover" plan. As I said, the first is a question of three months, the second of three years. What do you think of this yourself?"

I could do nothing more than show ignorance by shrugging my shoulders. "Naturally you Americans don't know the situation here, and it is hard to say which is the best method to use. But what do you think your backers will say?" Again I could give no answer. Hitler continued.

"You see I am not even clear myself, nor are my co-workers, which path we should take. Goring is simply for revolution, the others more for legal takeover, and I am in favor of both. Revolution can put power in our hands in a few days, legal takeover requires long months of preparation, and a lot of underground work. Of course there is a reason why we haven't been able to make a decision, and it is that we don't know how much money we can count on from your backers. If you had been more generous in 1929 things would have been settled long before this, but we were barely able to carry out half our program with ten million dollars. I will itemize our calculations for you. Revolution means we attract people by large donations to the unemployed, buy weapons quickly and organize our Storm—Detachments. Smugglers will take advantage of us and demand prices that will severely cut into our funds. With a lot of money we will certainly succeed in smuggling in machine guns, it makes no sense to open our attack without machine guns."

"Legal takeover on the other hand, when it has finally been completed, after we have forced different elections by obstruction in the Landtags and Reichstag, then the masses will be tired of voting and will be easily bluffed by our clever propaganda. While we take care of our parliamentary work we arm our people and organize the Storm-Detachments. Then a few repeated demonstrations from time to time against the Communists will be enough to give the people an idea of our armed power. In addition we will use the time to penetrate even deeper into the ranks of the Reichswehr. The elections, by giving us an effective majority, achieve the same result as revolution would in three or four months. I would like to have both ways. Everything depends on the money."

Hitler sat down at his table. He took out his little notebook, looked up at me, and continued.

"Revolution costs five hundred million marks, legal takeover cost two hundred million marks." He waited. "What will your backers decide?"

I couldn't answer. I promised to contact New York and report as soon as possible what they had decided. Hitler took up the conversation again and began to ramble.

"You people there in America must be interested in our party coming to power in Germany, otherwise you wouldn't be here and ten million dollars would never have been given to me in 1929. Your motives don't interest me, but if you understand the situation well you will surely realize that I can't get anywhere without financial means. The Communists here get money from Moscow, I know this and can prove it. The Social Democrats are supported by Jewish bankers and other large banks, and have a huge treasury. German Nationalists get huge sums from large industry, and their leader Hugenberg owns several newspapers that earn big profits. The Center Party gets whatever money it needs from the Catholic Church, which has billions at its disposal, especially in South Germany. When I compare that to the meager forty million marks I received from your backers in 1929, then I can hardly believe that we could have dared to start our planning with such limited funds. You must have noticed how we have progressed in Germany and here in Berlin since 1929. Aren't you amazed at these results? Should I tell you something else? The Reichswehr is National Socialist through and through. You know that already, but there is not one civil service our party does not have a strong following in, we are especially powerful in the railroads and Post Office, and when our revolutionary slogans are circulated in a few months we can put our hands on these state institutions without too much trouble. When I spoke to you in 1929 I had to admit that the North and Rhineland were still lukewarm. Now that is completely changed. We are well organized even in Frankfurt am Main, where German

Nationalists and Communists have a strong following. Party members are sitting in numerous foreign consulates, and will participate actively at the first signal from Berlin. Doesn't all this mean something? Doesn't it prove that those "paltry" forty millions were well invested? But everything now must go well and quickly, and our money is used up. Tell your backers that they should, in their own interests, send the five hundred million marks as quickly as possible, then we will be finished in six months at the latest."

Hitler screamed out these last sentences as if he stood at a political rally, and he assailed me as if I were his worst enemy. I had had enough. I repeated that I would report to New York and let him know as soon as I could. I telegraphed that same day. It took five days to receive an answer from New York. In those five days I had the feeling that I was never alone. Except, of course, during the hours I spent in my hotel. I thought I saw people everywhere who followed me. I still don't know if it was reality or my imagination, but I could think of several different occasions that are strong proof of a continuous control hanging over me in those five days. But I don't want to stir up the detective instincts of my readers. There is, however, one case I would like to relate. The second day after my conversation with Hitler I went on the Kurfurstendamm towards Wilmersdorf. An old friend of my family lived in a small villa there. I wanted to visit him. As I went down the Kurfurstendamm and turned into the street where the villa stood, I clearly saw a man pass in front of me whom I had noticed at least three or four times in front or behind in the last ten minutes. I arrived at the villa and was just about to press the electric doorbell when I saw a small box outside the bushes. Printed in pencil on it was the word: absent. I didn't ring. That evening I telephoned my friend's house from my hotel. I could get no connection, and after waiting several minutes the operator told me that no one was at home. This still seemed very normal and natural in Berlin, but later — I had written my friend a letter on my last day in Berlin and said how much I had regretted his absence — I received an answer from him in New York, in which he said he had not been away from Berlin, and could not understand my statement of his absence. I also didn't understand the story until I learned at the beginning of this year that our old family friend in Berlin was a well-known Social Democrat and had flown to Switzerland. We Americans are generally only mildly interested in the political persuasions of our friends. I had never known earlier that he was a Social Democrat, but now the incident in 1931 is clear, and I believe I was not only being shadowed personally in those five days, but my telephone and hotel room were also under control. We should not forget that in 1931 Hitler was not yet Reichskanzler, just leader of a strong political party.

Carter's answer was unclear. I wired back: "Repeat," and then received a long cablegram:

Suggested amounts are out of the question. We don't want to and cannot. Explain to man that such a transfer to Europe will shatter financial market. Absolutely unknown on international territory. Expect long report, before decision is made. Stay there. Continue investigations. Persuade man of impossible demands.

Don't forget to include in report own opinion of possibilities for future of man.

So Carter had no great belief in Hitler's financial capabilities. He would wait for a detailed report from me before making a decision and expected me to convince the Fuhrer of the impossibility of his demands, and to include my own opinion on the chances for success in the report.

I wrote Hitler a short letter and described the content of the telegram. Two days later two men I hadn't met yet, Goring and Streicher, visited me in my hotel. The first was an elegant-looking man, dashing in appearance, very brutal, and the second made a feminine impression on me.

Goring opened the conversation by expressing his amazement that I did not share the opinion of the

Fuhrer. It would certainly be difficult as an American to understand the German situation, but the Fuhrer had informed me so well of the plans and platform of the party, that I should be well on top of the situation. I countered immediately that my views were irrelevant, I was not the one with the money, but just a middleman. He didn't seem to believe this, and continued to speak to me in a personal way, denying the fact that I had backers behind me. Streicher entered the conversation with an unctuous tone. I could not stand the man. I preferred Goring's brutality a hundred times over, however unpleasant it was. We couldn't agree. I explained I don't know how many times that I could change none of the circumstances, that I had sent off my report to New York that same day and had to wait for my backers' decision. Goring finally became furious and said literally: "This is all a swindle. We didn't call on you. First you dangle a huge sum of money in front of our eyes, then when we tell you how much we need, it is much too high for you and the gentlemen don't come up with the goods. You are swindlers." This brutality made me mad and I showed Goring the door. He left with Streicher without saying good-bye. I immediately wrote a short letter to Hitler and requested him to deal with me personally in the future and not to send any more representatives, especially not Goring. I related briefly what had happened, and added that I wanted nothing more to do with Goring again. I don't know what transpired between Hitler and Goring, but the next day I received a short letter from Goring offering his apologies and blaming his behavior on the great tension he lived under being a party leader along with Hitler.

The next day, however, two men were announced again. Americans make a grave mistake in Europe. They receive anybody after a simple announcement. In America it makes no difference, everything is accomplished quickly. Superfluous speeches seldom take place in the business world there. I received the two men: von Heydt and a new figure. Introduction: Gregor Strasser. A more refined type than Goring, but equally brutal underneath a cover of formality. Von Heydt opened the conversation. I hardly listened and interrupted him. All this talk about party leaders made no sense at the moment. I had to wait for New York's decision. If Herr Hitler wanted the opportunity to speak to me, I would gladly discuss things with him and attempt to make the position of my backers clear. Strasser intervened. Did I share their point of view? "I have no point of view in the whole situation. I am carrying out an assignment. The answer they sent me was, however, left in code, and even though I passed it on to Hitler, it might be possible that I could explain certain points further. This is how my statement should be interpreted."

Strasser began to expound on the party platform. I had the impression that his job was mainly to work with the unemployed. He reproached, without being crude, however, the union bosses and the Social Democrats. He listed forty, fifty names one after the other and pointed cold-bloodedly to the wall, saying quietly: "This is where those fellows will be standing with ten sharpshooters in front of them." The coarsest words he used were rascal and dog, but he uttered these as calmly as everything else. I had had enough of this chatter and asked the men to leave me alone, as I had still a number of letters to write. Strasser gave me an invitation to attend a National Socialist parade in Breitenbach the following Sunday.

An overwhelming sight. On a field with gnarled tree stumps stood five Storm—Detachments in formation, listening to the priest who held the field service. I have remembered the following sentences from the priest's sermon. They gave me a much clearer understanding of German National Socialism than all the words of Hitler and his leaders.

"You are fighters for God. Day in, day out the best blood will be spilled because you have heroically put up your lives as bulwarks against Bolshevism, to save 2,000 years of Christian culture from ruin. You, you have inscribed the bitter fight for German nature and race on the red flag of the people with its white field of purity and loyalty and the runic sign of victory, you are satisfying your own consciences as well as God's. Do not let yourselves be led astray, and do not be intimidated."

"The spirit of Christ is the spirit of conflict, against Satan and against his hell. The enemy that Christ wanted to conquer by his crucifixion aspires to rise again right at this moment, the enemy, the eternal Wandering Jew, has decided to take revenge. He endeavors to destroy the holiness of marriage, and to poison the purity of custom and the soul of the people on purpose. Christian brotherly love must be brought into the battle, because the existence or nonexistence of Christianity is at stake. Comrades, our battle is a vital defense, our nationalism is the savior of people and fatherland. Do not listen to the politicians who designate our fanatic nationalism as misdeed, condemning al_ nationalism. Our nationalism is the same as that of a Pastor Wetterle, as that of a Cardinal Mercier von Mecheln, of Cardinal Dubois in Palis, who with thousands of their priests inflame the French people to a burning love of their country and encourage stamina for victory with glowing enthusiasm. What is good enough for the French and Belgians is equally good for us Germans. In the burning world of 1914 the enemy stood at the German borders, today the enemy rests in the core of our country, subjugating our people and enslaving it. In August 1914 millions, blessed by the church and protected by the prayers of the church, went to the murderous battlefields to save people and fatherland. What was permitted then, even demanded of our priests, should now be forbidden as evil teaching? ... Comrades, that is a lie. So I say to you, to be National Socialist is to be a fighter for a people that is prepared to defend its religious beliefs, its purity of custom, and its honor to the last breath. You are a providence of God, because you want to banish the underworld with its deadly poison of dissension.

The blessing of God rests on your battle. And now let us remove our helmets. Let us fold our hands and sing, as the Dutch Geusen did before the last decisive battle, so that it will ring a thousand fold all over the land: Lord make us free…"

The prayer of thanks is over. The field service is at an end. Sharp commands ring all over the field. The brown rows line up to march off.

Two policemen in green uniforms watch the Storm-Detachments with interest. The police are all at their posts. They had strict orders to watch all movements of the Storm-Detachments all over Germany, especially in Prussia. Secretary of the Interior Severing spoke last week in the Reichstag about these dangerous preparations for takeover by the NSDAP[4]. Three days later I received a cablegram from New York: "Report received. Prepared to deliver ten, maximum fifteen million dollars. Advise man necessity of aggression against foreign danger."

I wrote to Hitler again to arrange a meeting. I told him that I had received word from New York and that I preferred to inform him of its contents personally. That same evening von Heydt, accompanied by Strasser, visited me. "The Fuhrer is overworked. Upon the advice of his doctors, he must

---

[4] National Socialist Party.

have at least two weeks of rest." They had full powers to act in his name, for which they had proof. Reluctantly I described the contents of the telegram from New York.

Von Heydtsaid: "Fifteen million dollars" — he chose the maximum immediately — "is not much for our massive plans, but I know the Fuhrer will accept it. Now there can be no talk of revolution. It is not as easy as Goring and the others imagine. I would even gladly go out on the barricades myself. I have had enough of these conditions. But we can't put foolish ideas in our heads. We would be shot down before we knew what happened. That would be irresponsible to our Fuhrer. Now we must go to Hitler with proposals to organize ourselves more efficiency and to train our people. To have a revolution now would show a lack of soldierly and comradely spirit, provoking sacrifice is a communist idea. We will have nothing to do with that. Sending the Storm-Detachments to the barricades now would mean the destruction of our movement, would spill blood, valuable blood for nothing, and the flag of chaos and desperation, the flag of Bolshevism, would be planted on our dead bodies. In the past few weeks we have had an influx of new elements in our party that are even harder to handle, they come from other parties and have other viewpoints, and they have to adapt to our world."

Von Heydt, just like all other leaders of the National Socialist party I have met, seemed to be possessed by a mania to broadcast, either rightly or wrongly, the platform and tactics of the party as if he were at a political rally.

Strasser asked me when I thought the fifteen million dollars could be paid out to Germany. I answered that it was a question of a few days, as soon as I knew that Hitler agreed with the determined amount, but I would only take the necessary measures to sign the amount over to Europe when I had had a discussion with Hitler. Von Heydt explained to me that this was temporarily impossible because Hitler had to have rest. To wait for his return would mean great delay. If I insisted upon it then tomorrow or the next day a meeting of all party leaders could be organized, and I could report there what I wanted to say to Hitler personally. I kept, however, to my demand and said finally that I would do nothing until I had spoken to Hitler personally.

The next day at noon I was called away from lunch in my hotel. A chauffeur awaited me in the hall and gave me a letter. It was written in Hitler's handwriting, and it requested me to come to his house in the automobile waiting there. A quarter of an hour later I sat in his room on the Fasanenstrasse. I noticed neither fatigue or sickness on him, but said nothing of his health, just carried out my assignment directly. Hitler stood up, and while he walked up and down the room he shrieked: "Fifteen million dollars, that is about sixty million marks. How long will it be until it gets here? It is much too little to really tackle the problem. You Americans don't know our plans."

I remarked that fifteen million dollars was the maximum, and he could tell from the copy of the cablegram I showed him that ten million and a maximum of fifteen million were offered. He listened at first attentively. I took the opportunity to refer to the necessity of an aggressive stance towards foreign countries as mentioned in the cablegram. Supposedly America had the impression that his actions in other parts of Europe had not really had effect. I didn't want to go any further. Perhaps he would realize what my backers meant. But Hitler began to shriek again. "Do you think I can perform miracles here with our people? Do you have any idea of the apathy of the Germans? This 'pack of Jews' has imposed a spirit of swindling, acquisitiveness, internationalism, and pacifism. Day in, day out we must fight it: first we must teach the people courage, then we can do something."

"There is no discipline in Germany, and we must start from the very beginning again. Just wait until we are finished without work on the German people, then we can think about foreign policy. Read our platform. We will not stray from it one inch. Read points 1 through 7. Point 1. Establishment of a unified national state, including everyone of German origin. The explanation of this runs: we will not give up one single German in the Sudentenland, in Alsace-Lorraine, in Poland, in the League of Nations colony of Austria and in the succession states of old Austria. Read the explanation to point

2: we don't want Erzberg's and Stresemann's servility towards foreign powers; soon it will be seen that foreign powers will have much more regard and respect for a strong representation of German interests. The result of our new stance will be consideration and attentiveness to German wishes on foreign and international territory instead of kicks and beatings. Point 3 says: removal of Jews and all non-Germans from all responsible positions of public life. And Point 4? Immigration of Eastern Jews and other inferior foreigners will no longer be permitted. Unwanted foreigners and Jews will be turned away from the country. Read Point 6 again: whoever is not German can only live in the German stare as a guest and is subject to laws pertaining to aliens. Point 7: rights and interests of Germans supersedes rights and interests of foreign citizens. Above all we have as our goal the rebirth of Germany in the German spirit for German freedom. What more can you want? We will adhere to this program and will fulfill it to the last letter. I know that I will have France, Poland, Czechoslovakia, maybe also Prussia, Italy and Hungary on my neck because of this. That is irrelevant at this point. We will deal with that once our people are prepared to take on the consequences of German politics in the interest of the German people, with no reservations. The people have become bastardized and foreign customs must be driven out of them." Hitler sat down again and thought. Then he spoke more calmly.

"Good, I will take the fifteen million. We will

carry out our program, but our tactics will change. I will choose the slow path, the path of legal takeover, but we will succeed. A change is already coming over President Hindenburg. I will be finished when I have moved the aristocratic clique that surrounds him out of the way. His son thinks nothing of me and incites his father against me. The president is an old man. He lets others influence him. Just give me the fifteen million. Von Heydt will make the arrangements with you as to how I will receive the money."

I explained further that it was possible my backers would send the fifteen million in two installments, one of ten million and later one of five million, and they would wait for information from me before doing anything. I referred once more to the meaning of the conditions in Carter's telegram — a vigorous foreign policy. This time he didn't preach the standard phrases about his platform, but said directly and quietly: "Just leave it to me. What I have achieved already is proof of what I can do in the future."

The conversation had come to an end, which pleased me very much, a conversation with Hitler is an exhausting thing. He yells and raves at you. Obviously he is so used to speaking at national assemblies, it takes hold of him so, that he can't carry on a normal, quiet conversation.

That same day I wired a detailed report of my conversation with Hitler to New York and referred for the moment only to his plans for foreign policy and his firm promise not to stray an inch from his party platform. I didn't think this would be enough to satisfy Carter and his colleagues regarding an aggressive foreign policy by the National Socialists, and thought the deal would be closed.

Three days later I received an answer from Carter that contradicted my opinion. Fifteen million dollars would be delivered upon my first request to a European bank indicated by me. I promptly gave this answer to Hitler. Von Heydt looked me up and asked me to transfer the money to Europe immediately in the following way: Five million dollars in my name to Mendelsohn & Co., Amsterdam, five million to the Rotterdamsche Bankvereinigung, Rotterdam, and five million to the Banca Italianna in Rome.

I traveled to these three places with von Heydt, Gregor Strasser and Goring, to deposit the amounts. A huge number of checks had to be made out to many different names in large and small locations in Germany. The National Socialist leaders had long lists of names with them. In Rome we were received in the main building of the bank by its President-Commissioner, and while we waited in his office for five minutes two fascists whose uniforms obviously indicated high ranks came in. Introduction: Rossi and Balbo.

Goring opened the conversation. He spoke Italian to the men. I couldn't understand what was said. We were invited to a dinner at Balbo's house. I was the only one not in uniform. The National Socialist leaders wore their brown uniforms and the fascists their black ones. After dinner everyone danced in a huge hall, with open doors looking out on a magnificent garden. The brown uniforms were much preferred by the ladies. An old Italian, a black-shirt with many decorations, sat next to me and watched the dancers. He began speaking in German. "Italy should never have given up its alliance with Germany. Then we would be in a much stronger position against France. But our German friends are on the right path, and when revolution becomes reality then the good old days will come back. There is no better combination possible: Italian culture with German spirit, they will renew and conquer the world." Three days later I traveled on the Savoya from Genoa to New York.

Carter called a full meeting the next day after my return from Europe. Rockefeller asked immediately if I thought Hitler would dare an open battle with Hindenburg. I said that I felt Hitler to be capable of anything if it would further his goals. He was also no dreamer and was very aware of difficulties he faced, he would not experiment if he was not sure of success. I was asked to quote what was said in my dialogues with Hitler literally. I was also questioned on my impressions of conditions in Germany. When I gave the opinion of the Hamburg banker, Glean wanted to know if well-to-do classes in Germany feared Hitler's financial policies and his "breakdown of the enslavement of finance capital" as Hitler called it. I answered by quoting the Berlin industrialist and the feeling of the Hamburg banker, that points can be found in every political platform that are only there to please the masses, and will never be put into practice. I formed the conclusion that the wealthy German classes (according to Hitler's wishes) would not take these aspects of the Hitler program seriously. Carter remarked that the requested amounts I had wired were absurd and proved clearly how little understanding Hitler had of international relations. I added that in my opinion this was not only the case with financial relations, but I had also been amazed at his ignorance in the area of international politics. No one seemed to find this significant — it is quite common in America. Carter asked me what I thought about Hitler's co-workers. I related the incident with Goring. This seemed to please him especially, and he said flatly that a man of Goring's type would be a fitting partner for a leader like Hitler.

A full year later, in September, after the National Socialist Party in Germany received 107 delegates in the Reichstag on the 14th, Carter wrote me a short letter, recalling my two trips to Germany and the conversations I had had with Hitler. He asked me if I was prepared to go to Germany again to have a meeting with the Fuhrer in case it was necessary. After my last visit to Germany I had received letters regularly from von Heydt, Strasser, and Goring, along with extensive shipments of books, brochures, and daily newspapers. I was now very familiar with National Socialism, and the person of Hitler was no longer as mysterious to me through my contact with him as it was for others in our circles. To see these people again in Europe was not the most pleasant prospect. Neither the people nor their literature or propaganda held much to attract me. Perhaps my German origins have faded into the routine of American life. My grandfather came to America ninety years ago, my father was born there, my mother is pure American. Perhaps for that reason I could not stand the inflated arrogance of the German people, which was the key to Hitler's whole program, and his work and goals were completely alien to me. In fact, I had personally come to the conclusion that my friends were on the wrong path, that Hitler's aggressive foreign policy might well make France more flexible and cooperative, but it was also dangerous for the world. It is always well known where such a dictator begins, but no one ever knows where it all ends. I had told Glean during the course of the year of my viewpoint, and he tried to dissuade me with the information that Mussolini, an equally violent dictator of a large country, had cooled off after having caused anxiety in the world and especially in France with his big mouth and threats, which was very good in his opinion, but when the going began to get rough, (Mussolini) retreated calmly. It would be no different with Hitler, he thought. It was certainly not our intention to cause war between Germany and France, but just to threaten the danger of war, to make France cooperate more in the possible support of England and America in international financial affairs.

I finally made my decision. I informed Carter that I was prepared to travel to Europe again and to deal with Hitler as soon as it was necessary.

In the sleeping car to Berlin I found an edition of a German daily newspaper. This was the main article on the front page;

People are streaming in masses from the inner city towards the Jahrhunderthalle, and the surrounding squares and buildings for the assembly on the fairgrounds. Buses, trucks, private cars and motorcycles are being parked in the nearest streets. To the left of the autos run streetcars crammed with people, and impatient women and men have waited since three o'clock with folding chairs and food parcels in front of the entrance to the building. By five o'clock the bridges over the Oder leading to the fairgrounds are black with people and autos. Traffic is being strictly controlled, but stoppages are still taking place. Cries of "Heil" keep ringing when vehicles carrying party members and Storm-Detachments, singing and displaying flags, arrive at the meeting places. Police walk around with lunch bags and water bottles. It is said that their squad cars are riddled with machine guns and tear gas bombs. Special trains run one after the other into the stations. Happiness, enthusiasm, bliss on all faces of women and men, workers, peasants, citizens, officials, students and unemployed, all are caught up in the excitement that adds to the inner suspense of the huge election campaign. Unforgettable, wonderful day. Hitler will speak.

For the first time the whole SA of the province will march. There are Storm-Detachments among them who have sat in open trucks for ten hours or longer before reaching the meeting place. The SA columns are showered with flowers, it becomes a triumphal parade. Raised arms greet each other constantly. Heil SA, Heil…Drums roll, horns sound.

A crowd of thousands mills around in the gigantic concrete building of the Jahrhunderthalle, the massive memorial reminding the Prussian people forever of the great days of 1813. Long banners are draped on the ramparts and arches of the second largest domed building in the world. Written there is: "We don't fight for mandates, we fight for our political ideology." "Marx ism must die so Socialism can live." There is no place in this world for a cowardly people." "Attention, Attention," sounds from the loudspeaker. "Everyone sit down, the SA is marching in."

And they close in. The huge building trembles. A roar like a hurricane breaks forth, twenty thousand people rise from their seats. Between shouts of joy banners and flags are raised, one covered with black. A mother screams. An unknown storm— trooper has died a hero's death for his people. The Storm—troopers march in.

They can already be heard singing outside: "We are the army of the swastika." Enthusiasm reaches the boiling point. More columns keep coming. Men who know nothing more than duty and battle. The floor shakes under the marching feet, under the strength and discipline of the brown battalions.

"Attention, Attention, Hitler has just arrived. Attention, Attention." Excitement everywhere. "Heil, Heil." He comes, thousands of eyes look for the Führer. There he is. Sharp commands, a joyful cry: "Adolf Hitler." Now silence. The Gauleiter steps up to the microphone: "My dear German comrades," he begins. After a few sharp sentences he closes: "The Fuhrer will speak."

Again a giant roar, then the masses listen. Adolf Hitler speaks. First slowly, measured, and cool. The first applause. Hitler nods for silence. He continues to speak with more conviction, irresistible, he becomes fervent and demanding, the non-National Socialists are struck. What this front-line soldier lieutenant first class

Adolf Hitler, this man of the people, says is all so simple, so ordinary and so right, and everything so true, that know-it-alls, boastful of their development, and rational ones with their eternal practical complaints, are all silent. They follow the speaker with suspense. They have trouble understanding this man, whom they have come to see out of curiosity, but they applaud him.

Hitler indicates silence. "Those who belong to us know that a turning point in the history of our people happens not every five or ten years, but perhaps only once in a century…" Now he shrieks loudly: "Party platforms are worthless." Those people standing on the sidelines, the disappointed, the ones who have been betrayed so many times, listen carefully.

"Thirteen years ago we were broken as a people, and a broken economic life followed the broken people. Once, a hundred years ago at that time the ones who brought new prosperity and happiness to the German people were not those who

only thought of the economic life, but those who gave blood and possessions for the honor of the German people. It cannot be otherwise. The German economic life is not broken, the German people are…" The front-line soldier Hitler is not speaking of platforms, but of sacrifice, submission and work.

Now his voice sounds like a drum roll, now he speaks of Germany, and how. Hearts are inflamed, what a testament, a will and a belief as strong as rock. Hitler loves Germany, he loves and fights alone for Germany, always only for Germany.

Eyes are shining, faces are resolute. The doubtful become courageous, disbelievers begin to hope, the indifferent and apathetic are taken up with him, and old soldiers are inspired to new deeds. Hitler attracts them all into the circle of his mastery with his glowing will to freedom. An enslaved people wakes up, class distinctions fall away, no class-conscious workers and discontented citizens, no, twenty thousand comrades believe and shout with joy, believe in the Fuhrer and acclaim him. —

I read all this in the sleeping car on the way to Berlin. I also read that von Pfeiffer had been dismissed by Hitler, that von Heydt had stepped down from the party, and that Strasser had been left cold because his brother had incited mutiny among the Storm-Detachments.

I am almost glad that I accepted the assignment to meet Hitler for the third time. Things are happening in this country that we only know through reading past history. So very few have actually been charged with being there, standing in the middle of things, speaking to the Fuhrer and learning his most secret motives.

A strange atmosphere hangs over Berlin. Whether it is the calm before a storm? I don't know. No one speaks of politics. I visited the old friend in Wilmersdorf. His house is abandoned, this time I can tell that he was really not there. I have a conversation with the manager of a big department store. He reveals nothing of the situation. To all my questions he only answers that hard times are coming, and I could get no more from him. In several areas of Berlin the city looks strange, policemen next to stockpiles of rifles and machine guns. Open trucks full of Reichswehr soldiers race by at insane speeds, through the quiet streets. Motor brigades fly over the Kurfurstendamm, armed troops can be seen everywhere around government buildings near my hotel. Few brown uniforms. An odd phenomenon, to my mind. Hitler has, after all, been taken into the government. The few newspapers daring to raise the question speak of him as the chancellor of the future, a very near future. I had expected more demonstrations of power from the Hitler party in Berlin. I learned nothing from newspaper reports. A great deal was clarified, however, when I talked to an attaché of the American embassy. He told me that Hitler had already put clamps on the press even though he was not yet chancellor, that his Storm-Detachments (SA) were mobilized to take over the city at the first signal, that the appearance of the Reichswehr, even though official, meant nothing, since the government could not use it against Hitler's troops, however much it might need to, because it was unreliable and contained many National Socialist elements; that Hitler had added a new group of fighters to his Storm-Detachments and troops that he himself named Murder-troops. Nobody in the other political parties protested this brutal designation, which is a challenge to civilization. The Social Democrats are broken because they realize that all their years of parliamentary work have led to nothing, the Communists are becoming afraid even though it was they who yelled the loudest. Yesterday their Karl Liebknecht-house was taken by surprise and searched from cellar to attic. Officially it was done by police and Reichswehr, but my informant remarked that Hitler's Murder-troops had a large part in the destruction of the Karl Liebknecht-house. Many Communist leaders had already been taken prisoner, the red flag was forbidden, certainly only temporarily, but it would not be appearing before the elections. The Social Democrats are lukewarm in their manifestos and daily newspapers. Everyone feels that they are unable to cope with the situation. The German people want to be impressed, they only have respect for strong speakers. Germans are just children, naive people. They will never be attracted by an important principle.

First I received a brief summary of the political situation. My informant even risked a prediction. "Hitler can no longer be stopped," he continued. "You will see, next week he will be Reichskanzler. A von Papen can't fight it, a von Schleicher tried it with the help of the young Hindenburg, but he was unsuccessful. Hitler can be Reichsprasident if he wants. He will be satisfied with the chancellery only temporarily. But Hindenburg is old and something could happen any day, then Hitler will be a complete dictator without even the appearance of a constitutional head. Anything is possible with this man. I have spoken to him a few times and heard his speeches, and he does what he wants with his audience. He doesn't let them think, just screams and yells so they can't resist him anymore. When I listened to him I always had the feeling I had to fight the power of his suggestion, to keep from going along with him one hundred percent. When you ask yourself later what he said you can't remember it. What do you think of National Socialism?"

I didn't want to give him an answer, especially not a complete answer. "We should wait," I said, "we Americans ultimately have nothing to do with it. If the German people want to think of Hitler as their savior, then that is their privilege, it's not our business."

My confidant felt differently and tried to prove to me that Hitler was a danger to Europe just as Mussolini was, and that the Italian danger would be strengthened by the National Socialists extension of power in Germany and by a Hitler dictatorship.

That same evening I wrote to Hitler's old address in Berlin, saying I had arrived and requesting a meeting. That night the Reichstag building burned down. Goring came to my hotel at noon, more brutal than before, arrogant and authoritarian. He was accompanied by a newcomer, whom he introduced to me as Goebbels. Both were full of the burning. They swore at the Communists who had set fire to the building and tried to persuade me to the belief in their sacred right to wipe out the Communists down to the last man. I followed the same tactics as before and expressed no opinion. They would only answer my question of where and when I could speak to Hitler after they were done raging. The Fuhrer would receive me in the evening at eleven-thirty at the Fasanenstrasse. Goring would pick me up by automobile.

Hitler was very upset. To be merely upset, for him, would mean hysteria for someone else. He was always upset, in the true sense of the word. His greeting was barely polite. He raged about the Communists who had set fire to the Reichstag, he accused the Social Democrats of having had a hand in the fire, he called on the German people as if he had thousands in front of him. I can't reproduce the whole raving monologue here because I retained almost nothing of it. It had no coherence. He went on for a full half hour before he sat down at the table and began a more or less controlled discussion with me, constantly interrupted by accusations and anger at the Communists.

I had no idea what I was there at Hitler's for. The situation was like this. Carter had received a letter from Hitler, requesting him to send his former middleman immediately to Germany for a meeting. Carter had showed me the letter, and after my acceptance a few months ago, had asked me to go immediately to Berlin. Now I sat in front of Hitler, but had no idea of what he would ask or say to me. I waited calmly.

"I would like to inform you of the progress in our ranks. Since 1931 our party has tripled in size. There are detachments in which the number of unemployed far exceeds the number of employed. Various electoral campaigns have taken their toll of our funds. Now we are on the brink of electoral victory, I have had to clean up the party. Certain elements, even in leading positions, were unreliable. But that is all over now. Now we are concerned with being successful in our last step. The Communists have played their last card with the burning of the Reichstag. The Social Democrats have been more difficult to defeat in our latest assault. Also, we can't forget the German Nationalists, and they have money. We can't come into Berlin with our troops because although we feel secure of the Reichswehr, we are not certain of the general populace there, especially in the north and the Jewish quarter. We have drawn a ring around Berlin and I have concentrated three quarters of our party's troop strength in it. Just a few more days and the big day will be here, election day. We have to win this last initiative. Either by elections or by force. In case the outcome of the elections is not favorable, my plan is definite: to arrest Hindenburg, his son, von Schleicher, von Papen and Bruning, and keep them prisoner. We will also take the Social Democratic leaders prisoner. Everything has been calculated up to the smallest detail. But half of our Storm-Detachments have only billy clubs, and the troops have old-fashioned carbines. Near the German border in Belgium, Holland and in Austria there are huge weapons supplies. Smugglers give no credit. They demand scandalous prices. Of course they are aware of what is happening here and are prepared for eventualities. You can't negotiate with those fellows. They want hard cash, nothing else."

"I thought you would be here in Berlin sooner, then I could have calculated everything accurately. Now, at the last moment, we must act quickly. Long discussions won't help. What do you think your backers will do? Our money is gone. Will you continue to support us or not? Don't forget that we are fighting against Moscow, against the whole German heavy industry, against the Catholic Church and against the International. These are no enemies to underestimate. Our party funds have barely risen, although I did raise the membership fee to two marks and dues to one mark. There are too many unemployed persons we maintain for free and who have to be provided with uniforms and weapons. Things are better in the flat lands, there our people have carbines and hunting rifles. In the cities it is more difficult. What do you think? How much will your people give us?" I couldn't answer. Especially since I was not prepared for this question and had not discussed it with Carter before my departure.

"I have made no calculation, we had no time, and I don't trust my colleagues any more, but for a few exceptions. Our party has grown so much in such a short time that it has become more and more difficult for me to keep the leadership completely in my hands. That is absolutely necessary, since reliable leaders are very rare. The monarchists are beginning to come over to our side. Every day members of the Stahlhelm join up, sometimes in masses, and we can do nothing but welcome them, but we have to control the leaders who come along with them very strictly. I trust no one these days, I have finally made personal contact with Hindenburg. The conversation was anything but pleasant, the old man was very reserved, but I pretended not to notice it. I have time. He will know soon enough with whom he is dealing. When the day arrives he will either play along or disappear. I don't make compromises. You are no Jew are you? No, I remember, your name is German, yes, German origin. It is better for you to travel in Germany with a German pass. Goebbels can take care of it. You know him, surely. He, along with Goring, is one of my best partners. Von Heydt is no longer with us, you know that. Neither is von Pfeiffer. The Strassers are laughable. A mutiny in the SA against me, a full meeting of all the Gauleiter, and the incident was over. Strength, quick action, daring, are everything. Instead of acting quickly and not waiting, the Strassers and their people prepared and conspired in secret, and I was informed of all their activities when I stepped in at the last moment. They are weak brothers, overly politicized, with manners they took from the red rabble. What are they saying in America about the burning of the Reichstag?" Obviously he forgot that I was already here when the building burned. "But we know who the guilty ones are. We can prove everything. The Communist set fire to it, but behind him are both Communists and Social Democrats. They will regret it…" Hitler had slowly worked himself up to a frightening temper again and was now walking up and down in the room. Suddenly he ran to the door, pulled it open wide and looked into the hall. He began to rage and swear at someone who must be standing on the step. But I could see no one. I don't know what he was trying to do with his yelling. First I thought he wanted to prevent someone in the hall from hearing our discussion. But that wasn't the case, because when he came into the room again he continued to rage against the invisible person over something that was not clear. Perhaps it was the long wait for unimportant details, or over his inability to trust his subordinates.

He sat down again and said to me: "You have not mentioned the sum of money yet." There are moments when Hitler gave the impression of a sick man. It was always impossible to carry on a normal conversation with him. Sometimes his jumps from A to Z were such a hindrance and so stupid that his mental balance was doubtful. I think he has a hypernervous nature. In the last few years his mind has been occupied with a single idea. He has lived under constant tension. Many would have broken down, but Hitler seems to have an incredibly strong nature. I don't believe, though, that he has great understanding. When I try to summarize all the conversations I have had with him, I come to the conclusion that he is not intelligent, but unusually self-centered and tenacious. That is, I believe, his strength. We can all recognize a person of this type in our own circles, who, often dumb and barely developed, sacrifices everything for an idea or a possession, and either wins or perishes because of it. This is how I see Hitler. Whether he will be a blessing or a curse for a people like the Germans, only the future will tell, but I do think the German people are the only ones in the world to tolerate a man with such massive influence. There are so many weak points in his person and his behavior that the man himself as well as his party would have long been mocked and ridiculed in other countries.

Knowing the man after various conversations I had with him, I also understand now why he can no longer be tolerated after his final victory, neither by Germans nor by foreign journalists. He is actually a danger to himself and to his party because he cannot control himself, he reveals everything, babbling about his plans without the slightest hesitation. This had struck me even at our first conversation. Of course, I had had the strongest references, my identity was secure, he could tell from every detail that he was dealing with someone who represented the strongest financial group in the world, but for me it was no proof of his statesmanship and political insight to be informed so straight-forwardly of his most secret intentions.

In 1933 this was certainly less dangerous than 1929 or 1931. But in both those years he was equally frank with me as in 1933. Also he couldn't get away from the Jewish problem. That was the central issue for him, the problem of the greatest importance for the German people. His ideas on this subject would be considered laughable by an American high school student. He absolutely denies all historical fact, and I believe he knows nothing about the modern concept of "race."

After his question, or actually his reproach, "You have mentioned no sum of money," he began to speak of the Jewish problem, and by God, he began to compare the German problem with the Negro problem in America. That was enough for me to form an impression of Hitler's understanding and insight. Both problems are in no way comparable. I will spare you these nonsensical comparisons of his.

It was already three o'clock in the morning and I still did not actually know what he wanted of me. So I made use of a small pause in his incoherent speech to ask him: "You spoke of a sum of money?"

"Yes, that is the problem. We don't have much more time. This is the situation. Are your backers prepared to continue supporting us? What amount can you get for me? I need at least one hundred million marks to take care of everything, and not to miss my chance of final victory. What do you think?"

I tried to make it clear that there could be no talk of such a sum, first of all because he had already received twenty-five million and second because the transfer of such a large amount in a few days from New York to Europe would certainly disturb the stockmarket. Hitler didn't understand this, and he said so directly. He was not familiar with such complicated details in banking. "If you have the money in America, then certainly it can be turned over to Germany. Telegraphically or something, it seems very simple to me." It was hopeless and a complete waste of breath to enlighten him in international finance. I concluded by promising to report our conversation to my backers and then to wait and see what their decision was.

"You will telegraph, won't you? Do it here, then

your telegram will be handled more quickly. Code? We can also help you, I will just telephone for you." Now I had to explain that I corresponded with Carter in a secret code and he demanded to know whether nobody could read this cablegram, not even the directors of the telegraph company? He was amazed and thought it was bad that private persons could telegraph each other without the government of the different countries being able to decipher their reports. He admitted that he had never heard of such a thing. It was about four-thirty when I got back to my hotel and I immediately began to construct my code telegram to Carter.

It was very strange to read the German press in those days. Of course, one was told that Social Democratic and Communist weeklies were still available, but the hotel boy that I sent out for them kept coming back with the well-known Berlin papers. The burning of the Reichstag building was believed to be without exception a Communist misdeed. I was never able to learn other opinions, even if they were available. I read other explanations in America and elsewhere, but if it is true that the Hitler party had a hand in the burning, then Hitler is the best actor I have met in five continents.

Goring and Goebbels are almost as good. His anger, his frenzy about the burning were either completely genuine or incredibly well put on, and even now, just thinking of that conversation, I can still feel the influence of those wild feelings. I noticed another strange thing in those days about Berlin. At street corners and squares I often saw ten or twenty brown uniforms with swastikas standing in a circle. For a quarter of an hour they cried: "Clear out the manure! Vote National Socialist!" Then they walked on, formed another circle and cried: "The latest egg the Jews have laid, that is the German State's Party!" At noon time I saw out of my hotel window forty brown uniforms standing in a circle, a half hour long they yelled in constant rhythm:

> Proletarian, wake up!
> If to fight for the freedom of German work
> Is what you want,
> If bread for wife and child
> Is what you want,
> Then Defend yourself, defend yourself
> Worker with mind and fist
> Vote List Nine.

I always had to think of Hitler when I saw these people. In Berlin they were called the propaganda "speaking-choruses."

Everything Hitler. Short sentences. Just speak, scream, yell, without protest from anyone. No one could get a word in edgewise. Certainly a new propaganda method. They have discovered new methods here at home in the area of voting propaganda, but I have never seen anything as suggestive as this, anything that has such an effect on the masses, and the first party to use it naturally gets control of the streets, because even if another party holds a speaking chorus in the same area it results in a scuffle — it can't be otherwise.

The rhythm and the constant repetition of the same words puts the speakers in a kind of ecstasy, and in this ecstasy they are capable of anything. I have seen these brown people, how they look up over the heads of the crowds, as if they see a better world and they revel in this image. The ecstasy could be seen right on their faces. Can a person still think logically in ecstasy? Psychologists are the ones to ask. Yesterday I read somewhere in a dissertation that fascism and National Socialism were a sickness, perhaps a sickness of the soul. But I am just rambling.

Carter wired me that he could give seven million dollars at most, that means five million would be turned over from New York to Europe to the given banks and two million would be paid personally to me in Germany by the Rhenania Joint Stock Co. Rhenania is the German branch of Royal Dutch in Dusseldorf. I sent this answer to Hitler and waited. The next day Goebbels was announced very early in the morning. He brought me to the Fasanenstrasse.

Hitler received me in the same room, Goring was with him. The conversation was very brief. Almost abrupt. I had the impression that the three men were not satisfied with the stipulations, and that they had to force themselves not to lash out against me. Everything went well, however. Hitler asked me to sign over the five million dollars to the Banca ltaliana in Rome again, and Goring would accompany me. The two million had to be transferred in fifteen checks of equal value, in German money, all in Goebbels' name. The meeting was then at an end. I left.

I carried out my assignment strictly down to the last detail. Hitler is dictator of the largest European country. The world has now observed him at work for several months. My opinion of him means nothing now. His actions will prove if he is bad, which I believe he is. For the sake of the German people I hope in my heart that I am wrong.

The world continues to suffer under a system that has to bow to a Hitler to keep itself on its feet.

Poor world, poor humanity!

For translation faithful to the original, Zurich,
February 11, 1947

Rene Sonderegger

Epilogue

The preceding report appeared in the period after the dating of the Forward, after October, 1933 (as a Dutch translation of the English original) in the form of a ninety-nine page book published by an old, respected, still existent firm in Amsterdam. This book did not reach a wide public, however, since it disappeared after a short time forever from the book market, if it had ever been on sale publicly at all. Only isolated copies seem to have reached the hands of a third person. The existence of the book is not disputed. What is disputed is its authenticity. The firm explains that this book represents a huge falsification, or forgery:

The translator, Schoup, came to us with an original letter from Warburg, therefore we believed the book as well as its author to be genuine. After the book came out we learned from various sources that a Mr. Sidney Warburg, from the house Warburg in New York, did not exist and that the book was a massive deception. We immediately called back all copies from book dealers and destroyed the whole edition. We don't know if Schoup still lives: unfortunately he was never pursued.

The preceding German text is the exact word for

word translation of the Dutch book edition.

Today, at the end of 1946, thirteen years after 1933, after the second World War and the downfall of the Third Reich, after the complete subjugation of the German people and after the Nurnberg trials against the highest ranking surviving Nazi leaders, and faced now by the threat of World War III, we feel obligated to publicize this text, unedited and uncut, in order to make way for an exact analysis of its contents and origin.

It is possible that this report is forged and that its contents are substantially untrue. It is possible that the report is forged, but that its contents are substantially true. It is possible that the report presents a mixture of fiction and truth. But it is equally possible that he report is genuine, or that it is substantially genuine, yet contains several deceptions that testify against its authenticity. Anything is possible. It is important to establish the truth about contents and origin.

We pose the question of the truthfulness of the report. What evidence is there that it is a forgery, i.e. that its contents are substantially false? If it is false, in whose interest and by whom was this forgery created? Can it be proven that the contents of the report are substantially authentic therefore true? Can it be ascertained what is true and what is false in it?

In any case it can be established that the report can be authentic and true, that its authenticity and accuracy cannot immediately be disputed. This proof will be demonstrated by the following facts available to us. The report names many concrete, commonly known occurrences and facts that are relatively easy to verify.

It is supposed that Sidney Warburg is the New York banker and writer James Paul Warburg, son of Paul Warburg, who was Secretary of State under Wilson. Sidney can be a pseudonym. James P. Warburg was born in Hamburg in 1896. In 1902 he came to America with his father. As a young man he is said to have spent several years in his uncle's business in Hamburg, mentioned in the report on p. 6. At the time of his supposed trips to Germany he was 33 to 37 years old. James P. Warburg was an American delegate to the London World Economic Conference in 1933, mentioned on p. 4. James P, Warburg wrote a great deal about economics and politics. For example a book of his appeared in 1940, after many precedents, called Peace In Our Time?, one year later another, Our War and Our Peace, in 1944 another, Foreign Policy Begins at Home. In 1942 a book of his verse appeared entitled Man's Enemy and Man. Ferdinand Lundberg calls him "politically aggressive" in his well-known book America's Sixty Families. James P. should dispute the authorship of the report ascribed to him. The American Warburgs came from the old Hamburg banking family of Warburg. Felix Moritz Warburg, the promoter of Zionism, was born in 1871 in Hamburg, went to the U.S.A. in 1894 and married there in 1895 a daughter of Jacob Schiff from the banking house Kuhn, Loeb and Co. Felix had four sons who can eventually come into question as authors of the report, if the evidence of Warburg authorship is actually accurate. The case is improbable, however, because nothing seems to predestine them for this role. Paul Moritz Warburg, father of James Paul, his only son, was born in 1868 in Hamburg, married a daughter of Salomon Loeb from the banking house Kuhn, Loeb & Co. in 1895 and settled, as mentioned above, in the U.S.A. in 1902. A relatively short time later he sat in Wilson's government. The oldest brother of Paul and Felix, Max M. Warburg, was born in Hamburg in 1867 and remained head of the Hamburg firm. With the marriage of the Warburgs into the New York bank Kuhn & Loeb, the Warburgs became the most important Jewish financial capitalist power.

The Warburg report contains several inaccuracies and errors that, at first glance, strengthen doubt in its authenticity. We would like to point out these places. On p. 2 the author wants to "describe briefly the state of American finance in 1929." But then he goes on to refer to incidents in the following years. The dissolution of the Darmstadt and National Bank, the Nordwolle crash, the crisis of the Austrian Kredit-Anstalt all took place in 1931, the payment of Young—Obligations in 1930. The amount of outstanding credits abroad the U.S.A. has, is given as 85 milliard dollars. This figure is much too high. American outstanding credits abroad were actually only 18 milliard dollars.

The title runs Three Conversations With Hitler. On p. 5 the author speaks of "four conversations." There were exactly three trips and five separate conversations with Hitler.

On p. 24 Carter's answering telegram reads: "Explain to man that such a transfer (of 200 to 500 million marks) to Europe will shatter financial market. Absolutely unknown on international territory." On p. 38 the author writes that "the transfer of such a large amount in a few days (one hundred million marks) from New York to Europe would certainly disturb the stockmarket." Without knowing too much about these financial transactions, this fear seems to us improbable.

On p. 30 the author mentions that the Nazis had received 107 delegates in the Reichstag on September 14,1932. That is wrong. The Nazis received 107 delegates in the Reichstag on September 14,1930, in 1932 they already had many more. On the same page the author writes: "My grandfather came to America ninety years ago, my father was born there." The father of the supposed author, Paul Warburg, was born in Hamburg and settled with his family in the U.S.A. in 1902.

The Nazi rally described on p. 32 applies to the Breslau election rally on March 1, 1933. Therefore it took place after the burning of the Reichstag and after Warburg's conversations with Hitler. The author must have read the report on his return trip from Berlin, not on the way there.

On p. 34 the author is reading in a German newspaper in February 1933 that "von Pfeiffer had been dismissed by Hitler and that (Gregor) Strasser had been left cold because his brother (Otto) had incited mutiny among the Storm-Detachments." On p. 37 he has Hitler saying at the same time — "von Pfeiffer is no longer with us. The Strassers are laughable. A mutiny in the SA against me, a full meeting of all the Gauleiter, and the incident was over." The reader gets the impression that the cases of von Pfeiffer and Otto Strasser had occurred very recently. Instead they happened in 1930. It is possible, however, that they took effect afterwards, and were mentioned again in conjunction with the Gregor Strasser crisis of early December 1932.

Perhaps the most obvious error is found on p. 34, where the author writes that Hitler has already been taken into the government, but is not yet Reichskanzler. The text on p. 35 also implies that in February 1933 according to the author von Papen, not yet Hitler, is chancellor. One can conclude from a sentence on p. 24 ("We should not forget that in 1931 Hitler was not yet Reichskanzler, just leader of a strong political party") that the author knows as he is writing the report in the summer of 1933 that Hitler is chancellor. The same can be taken from the phrase on p. 38 "after his final victory." Every school child in Europe knew in 1933 that Hitler became Reichskanzler immediately when he entered the government at the end of January, 1933 and he remained so until his death. Perhaps what helped create the error was the author's lively and accurate memory that Hitler was at first only nominally Reichskanzler, that von Papen & Co. did not want to give up actual power, and that the struggle for power within the government witnessed from up close by the author continued on until Hitler first seized total power in the summer of 1933. In general, the tension of the German struggle for power in February of 1933 is absolutely correctly described by the author.

It is possible that the report contains additional errors and inaccuracies like these. It is, however, doubtful that they speak for the forgery of the report as a whole. If we accept that the report is falsified, then it originates from a very clever forger who has deep insight into actual facts. Such a clever forger would not allow clumsy mistakes like that of the Reichskanzler or the misdating of the number of delegates, all of which could make the reader mistrustful from the beginning. Perhaps some of these mistakes were made on purpose so the authorship could be denied if necessary, like, for example, the assumption that the author's family had been in the U.S.A. for 90 years. In fact these errors and superficialities speak more convincingly for authenticity than for forgery. An American banker, belonging to the circle of men of the world, who is at the same time not lost in inner European affairs, does not twist and turn every word seventeen times over before setting it down, as a German professor would. He writes off the top of his head, freely from memory, unhindered by larger or smaller exactitudes in side issues. As long as the main points emerge sharply and clearly, and it cannot be disputed that they do. Finally the report contains not only these and perhaps other errors, but also a large number, a majority, of accurate and provable statements. In addition, it contains many profound and excellent observations that prove the author to be not an ordinary shoemaker but a well-read, experienced and knowledgeable mind with insight, explicable only by either high theoretical training or collected personal experiences from top levels. The report contains predictions that sounded improbable in 1933, but were confirmed by events since that time. Finally there is a marvelous admission from one who participated. Naturally Goebbels couldn't keep his big mouth shut. So he writes in his dairy "Von Kaiserhof zur Reichskanzlei" on February 20,1933: "We are raising a huge sum for the election (Reichstag election of March 5, 1933) that disposes of all our financial problems at one blow." Even if we don't know, of course, if Goebbels' jubilant exclamation applies to the supposed American money to be sent by Warburg, the timely coincidence of both events is still remarkable.

The Warburg report as a whole gives an extremely serious impression, genuine, lively and unbelievable. Descriptions of Hitler and the content of his conversations seem especially authentic and true, they agree with everything we know otherwise about the subject. After the errors have been pointed out, several especially relevant facts will be mentioned, along with comment.

From the beginning, the reference in the Forward to the conflict within the capitalist, the mixture of honesty, decency and corruption, proves great awareness, Marx, in Das Kapital, spoke clearly of this economic role, the double role of the capitalist.

The great businessman, who won't let himself be deceived by any phrase, appears in short, brief sentences like:

Money is power. The banker knows how to concentrate and manage it. The international banker carries on international politics...Whoever understands what was concealed behind the word "national" in the last few years and what is concealed there still also knows why the international banker cannot keep himself out of international politics. (p. 3)

The American banking world had never been enthusiastic about Wilson. Bankers and financiers viewed his idealism as good enough for the study, but unsuited to the practical, international world of business. (p. 4–5)

Look for the explanation in works on political economy, in examples of practical, international economy, in fat books on the subject containing much idiocy, all betray a complete lack of insight into reality. Political economists are, first of all, primarily academics. (p. 6–7)

Is he not right?

Carter and Rockefeller dominated the proceedings.

Carter is Morgan's representatives. Guaranty Trust belongs to the Morgan group. Morgan and Rockefeller, the uncrowned kings of the world, give the orders and hold the Hitlers like puppets on a string with their millions. Carter (father and son) are official figures in the leadership of the Morgan bank in Paris, which played a very large role in the financing of World War I and in the regulation of debts and reparations in the period between the wars. Is the man mentioned here perhaps identical with John Ridgley Carter, born in 1865, who married an Alice Morgan in 1887, was attached until 1911 to the American diplomatic service and since 1912 belongs to the leadership of the Morgan Bank in Paris? It fits rather well.

On p. 9 Hitler says: "We can't count on sympathy from the large capitalists yet, but they will have to support us when the movement has become powerful."

According to other widely held opinions that statements completely accurate. Hitler received the first large sums of money from foreign capitalists like Ford, Deterding, etc. Wealthy German capitalists treated him with reserve for a long time.

Only after he had already come to power did the majority follow him. But it was decisively foreign capital that made Hitler.

The views on foreign policy that Hitler held in 1931, according to the 1933 report, were substantiated by later events, as were, incidentally, his other predictions. His prediction of the Russian pact is the most amazing of all. On p. 20 Hitler says in 1931:

The German people must be totally self-sufficient, and if it doesn't work with France alone, then I will bring in Russia. The Soviets can't miss our industrial products yet. We will give credit, and if I am not able to deflate France myself, then the Soviets will help me.

This seemed completely crazy to Warburg at the time. That is why he added immediately:

I must make a small remark here. When I returned to my hotel I wrote this conversation down word for word. My notes are in front of me, and I am not responsible for their incoherence or incomprehensibility. If you think his views on foreign policy are illogical, it is his fault, not mine.

Falsification!?!

Hitler's evaluation of the German "Communists" on p. 22 is to the point:

The best people here in Berlin are Communists, their leaders complain to Moscow of their bad straits and demand help. But they don't realize that Moscow can't help. They have to help themselves, but are too cowardly for that.

The position of Jewish capitalists in relation to Hitler and his anti-Semitism, as it is described in the report, has also been proven by other sources.

I had a talk with a bank director in Hamburg whom I had known well in the past. (Very likely Warburg's uncle) He was quite taken in by Hitler...It was hard for me to take his opinion seriously, because he was a Jew. I needed an explanation, so I asked him how it was possible for him, as a Jew, to be sympathetic to Hitler's party. He laughed. "Hitler is a strong man, and that is what Germany needs." (p. 18)

Again I posed my question of how my informant, as a Jew, could be a member of the Hitler party. He passed over the question with a sweep of his hand. "By Jews Hitler means Galician Jews, who polluted Germany after the war."

Warburg's comic dismay when Hitler rightfully compared the Jewish question in Germany with the Negro question in America is equally believable, (p. 38)

An important sphere of fact, that can strengthen adequately the real possibility of the Warburg report's authenticity by analogy concerns numerous, uncontested statements about moral, political and financial support and promotion of Hitler and German National Socialism by foreign and especially American capitalists, scattered about in the literature of these times.

First of all, the case of Henry Ford can be mentioned. The American auto- mobile king was known in the twenties as the richest man in the world. At the beginning of the twenties he carried on an open, well-known alliance with the German anti-Semites as their patron-saint, supported by the book The International Jew, illustrated by him and written by White Russian anti-Semites. This book appeared in German published by the anti-semitic Hammer-Verlag. In a publisher's announcement he writes:

This book has long since taken its place in the armoury of every mentally alert German person. No other publication of similar scope that treats the Jewish question with intellectual reasoning can claim a wider circulation.

On January 19, 1923, the Hasler Nachrichten reports: Henry Ford is perhaps the biggest anti-Semite of our time.

On September 13, 1923 the Judische Pressenzentrale Zurich (Central Jewish Press, Zurich) writes:

The anti-semitic International is organizing itself. As the JOB representative discovered, this (anti-semitic) agitation (in Czechoslovakia) started about two years ago: immediately after the negotiations Henry Ford conducted with German politicians in Czechoslovakia. The kind of agitation going on in Czechoslovakia strengthens the suspicion that there is a central location for international anti-semitic propaganda, seeking to systematically, according to definite plan, incite an anti-semitic world movement.

On November 9, 1923, shortly after Hitler's beer hall putsch, the Vienna Arbeiter-Zeitung (Workers Newspaper) wrote that "it was well known that Henry Ford was spending large sums to stir up the anti-semitic movement in Europe."

The Judische Pressenzentrale Zurich reported on March 24, 1924: — "Attacks on Henry Ford in the American Congress."

In one of the last sessions of Congress, Congressman La Guardia delivered a sharp speech attacking Henry Ford, accusing him of spreading anti-Semitism in Europe. La Guardia explained: "Henry Ford's wealth, along with his ignorance, have made it possible for malicious people to conduct a vile campaign against the Jews. This is not only true in America, but in the whole world. This inhuman, unchristian, and evil campaign has reached the other shores of the ocean and we see its consequences in the pogroms of innocent, helpless

Jews in various parts of Europe. Refute this if you can!"

On April 25, 1924 Crispin wrote in the Berlin Vorwarts (Forward) under the tide: "Ludendorff and the Jews." —

To complete Ludendorff s character profile, the source of his wisdom about the Jews will be revealed. The source of his wisdom is, according to his own testimony, the book circulated under Ford's name: The International Jew.

In 1927 an attack appeared against the anti-Semites by C.A. Loosely: "The Evil Jews!" The author polemicizes mainly against the two literary leaders of anti-Semitism, Ford and Rosenberg. He uses the expressions "Ford and his swastika-confederates" (p. 57), "the German anti-Semites in alliance with Ford" (p. 60), "Mr. Ford and Mr. Rosenberg" (p. 33).

The following appeared in Upton Sinclair's book about Ford, the automobile king, that came out in German in 1938 published by Malik-Verlag, London:

The former editor of the Dearborn Independent (belonging to Ford) who had written the anti-semitic article, was now Ford's private secretary and press chief, controlling all his public relations. William J. Cameron had not changed his views one iota; on the contrary, he was in contact with *numerous anti-semitic agents in the whole world and connected them with Henry Ford...Ford's millions surrounded him like a prisoner with Nazi agents and fascist slanderers. They had already begun to work on him when the Hitler movement was still young, and had received $40,000 from him for a German edition of the anti-semitic brochure, the names of Hitler and Ford appearing together in the prospectus. Later on a grandson of the ex-Kaiser joined up with Ford, and by his help $300,000 flowed into the Nazi party. Henry Ford had huge factories in Germany, and it was no Utopian idealism that prompted him to fight the strikes in that country. — Then Fritz Kuhn entered the picture, Hitler's primary agent in America, the uniformed head of the German- American Bund, a semi-military organization. He moved his headquarters to Detroit and received a post in the laboratories of the Ford works. A new anti-semitic campaign was begun and the Ford factory swarmed with Nazis. (p. 248–249)*

The German Hitler movement grew and took strength from 1920 on under the direct, open and close participation of Ford. Only when Ford's public support was no longer necessary did he separate himself from anti-Semitism. He continued to aid Hitler, however. The latter conferred an order on him after his takeover. The Volksrecht (People's Rights) reported on September 19, 1945:

The Ford works are accused of furnishing supplies regularly to the Nazis. The correspondent from TASS Agency in New York reports: "Documents discovered in Germany, as well as thorough investigation have proven that the American Ford Co. produced war materials for the Nazis and assisted German armaments before and during the war up to 1944. Before Pearl Harbor, Henry Ford himself approved the contracts between his factories and the Hitler government…In 1939 a gift of 50,000 marks is said to have been turned over to Hitler from representatives of the Ford works."

The American origin of European fascism is also evident in a report from the Judische Pressezentrale Zurich of December 22, 1922:

One of the leaders of the Ku Klux Klan explained in a conversation with journalists that the KKK had made all the preparations to expand into a world organization…in a very short time a branch organization would be founded in Canada, while trusted agents were being sent at the same time to Europe to create a KKK organization in various European countries. It would not last long and the movement would cover the whole world.

The European KKK did come to life in the form of fascism and National Socialism.

Occurrences in Bavaria in 1923 provide very interesting and significant information about foreign financial sources of the Nazis. Foreign impetus and interests behind the Nazis are easier to pinpoint in the beginnings of the movement because they were not as pronounced then, and methods of disguise were not yet well-developed. Events in Bavaria prove that foreign powers and interests were involved in the fascist movement from the very beginning, wishing to guide it according to their desires.

In March, 1923 a monarchist takeover in Bavaria was attempted by Fuchs, Machhaus & Co. The Vienna Arbeiter-Zeitungwrote on June 24, 1923:

The trial (against Machhaus & Co.) has, to begin with, established with completely unshakable evidence the French government's financing of the fascist movement. It was incontestably proven and confirmed by all witnesses that more than one hundred million marks were given by the French agent Richert to the fascist organizations in the second half of last year... France has invested its money well in the German Nazis, Millerand and Hitler are playing conveniently into each other's hands!

On July 10, 1923 the same newspaper writes on the affair again:

In clarifying the verdict it was explained that...the money at his (Richert's) disposal was intended to finance a takeover in Bavaria and the overthrow of the German Reich...Richert was working under assignment to the French government, and if his power seizure had succeeded he would have had to appear in court as the primary defendant along with the French government…The attempt to overthrow the German government by Richert- Fuchs-Machhaus was a highly official destructive undertaking by the French government against the political stability of the German nation and thereby against the national unity of the German people. The French government planned to carry out this overthrow in close coordination with the other French actions in the Ruhr. French armies on the Rhine and on the Ruhr had orders to begin marching from Frankfurt to Hof at the moment of the Bavarian putsch, thereby dividing the German north from the German south. The Bavarian overthrow would then be the pretext for the occupation of the Main river through France, and the French government would hope for further advantages from the success of separatist campaign efforts in Bavaria.

This is the plan of action of World War II in a nutshell. Only the real model for Fuchs-Machhaus is Hitler, for France is America and for Richert is Warburg. Hitler also had French money in 1923. His leader of the Storm-Troopers, Ludecke, had armed and invested one Storm-Detachment of the Munich Hitler—Guard with uniforms at French costs, but soon afterwards, to Hitler's sorrow, was discovered by the police with huge sums in franks and exposed. (See Vienna Arbeiter-Zeitung) of March 19, 1923). But Hitler not only had franks, he had surprising amounts of dollars in the inflationary times of 1923. Was his unusual strength perhaps the result of the possession of so many dollars? The Vienna

Arbeiter-Zeitung asked on April 15, 1923: "Shouldn't names like Ford, the American patron of anti-Semitism, be found under the gift-happy German Nazis living abroad?"

On February 17, 1923, the Vienna Arbeiter-Zeitung reported the following story under the title: "The Hitler with the Dollars."

What a shame for the Nazis. First it was proven that they received money from the French. Then one of their leaders is unmasked as a French spy and arrested. Now the Munchner Post is in a position to prove that even Hitler, well-known Nazi general, is in possession of a surprisingly large number of dollars. Our Munich party newspaper writes: Shortly before the National Socialist Parteitag Hitler appeared at a Munich business office in the company of his 'bodyguard' to buy furniture for the editorial offices of the Volkischer Beobachter (People's Observer) a new Nazi sheet. After the Parteitag the business owner went person— ally to the offices of the Volkischer Beobachter to collect the amount. Hitler was in the process of opening the mail. He removed huge sums in dollars from several envelopes sent to him. He paid the amount of five million from a briefcase stuffed with dollar bills. The somewhat amazed face of the businessman obviously must have prompted him to give an explanation for this, after all, quite unusual situation. He said off the top of his head: "The old fuddy-duddies always want to know where we get our money. You see, Germans living abroad support our movement. If we had to rely just on contributions from industrial magnates, then we would have needed long ago to get help from Germans living abroad." Mr. Hitler, then, has as you can see large amounts of money in foreign values at his disposal. The twisted explanation he felt he owed to the businessman, that the money came from Germans living abroad, is just a way out of an embarrassing situation. The money comes from abroad, and the hardly contested fact that the National Socialist party is fed through foreign channels is thereby firmly established.

In the Munich Hitler trials of 1924 it was determined that Hitler received $20,000 from Nurnberg industrialists for his putsch. Nothing annoyed Hitler as much as the accusation that he was being financed by foreign capitalists. For that reason, during the course of his rise to power in 1933 he would bring libel actions against those who aired such opinions. Since the accused could naturally not produce receipts and written corroborations, and the courts protected Hitler, and since in addition former participants and witnesses who had turned against the Nazis were cruelly persecuted by their former friends, Hitler emerged regularly as the victor from these trials, if he didn't prefer just to let them run themselves out. Such a trial took place in 1923 in Munich. The Vienna Arbeiter-Zeitung wrote on June 23, 1923:

Lantag delegate Auer declared as witness he had received the information that sums of money, one of them thirty million marks, had been transferred three times from the Saar territory to the Deutsche Bank, and had reached the possession of people who had otherwise not had any money to dispose of. There had been evidence proving that the money originated from Ford, the automobile factory owner, who played a large role in the National Socialist Workers Party, and was one of the authorities in the French iron syndicate. — Shopkeeper Christian Weber, member of the National Socialist party leadership, declared that the party certainly did get money from abroad, largely from party members in Czechoslovakia and from friends in America.

A similar trial took place against the writer Abel in Munich in the summer of 1932, therefore shortly before Hitler's power takeover. The Imprekoor of June 14, 1932 reported the following:

Hitler and some of his people who entered the battle as witnesses, tried their best to be vague and reveal nothing. The courts even came to Hitler's assistance in these efforts. Yet the trial did, in certain ways, explain things... The focal point of the trial was the interrogation of Hitler, which took place under sensational circumstances. The leader of the Brown House was obviously concerned with exploding the proceedings, to avoid embarrassing questions. He actually succeeded in slipping away at the right moment thanks to a true attack of delirium (even with foam on the mouth!)... He escaped scot-free when the question of foreign financial sources came up. He did, though, condescend to the ambiguous admission that the NSDAT had always been supported by its members abroad; therefore Germans abroad and naturally also Nazi patrons in Germany could be the channels through which money from Deterding, Schneider-Creuzot and Skoda could have flowed. But when the lawyers asked Hitler completely straight forward questions, he began to scream like one possessed, to insult the lawyers and refuse testimony. Even the Munich court, normally so favorable to him, could not get away from fining him 1,000 marks for "abusive behavior" and refusal of testimony, which could hurt Hitler. — Hitler's denials and raging are highly transparent. He has already been exposed on the one issue to which he responded, and he can even be suspected of perjury. He explained that he had never seen or spoken to the Italian Migliarati, who, according to Abel's assertion, is suspected of turning over sums of money to him. Meanwhile it was already proven in the Bayrischen Courier that Migliarati publicized an interview with Hitler at a critical point. It is now completely understandable why Hitler let it come to a denial of testimony and then left Munich in a hurry. Answers to numerous, very precise questions from the defense would have shed a great deal of light on Hitler's financial sources, on actions a leader can actually get away with, but which the rank and file will not tolerate.

The Neue Zurcher Zeitung also felt the same way, that Hitler verified Abel's accusations rather than disproved them by his unusual behavior in court.

The strong financial connections between Sir Henry Deterding, head of the Royal Dutch Petroleum Co., and Hitler are well known and still fresh in the memory so that it is enough just to mention the name here. Konrad Heiden writes on this matter in his Hitler biography: "Direct and indirect financial connections to Henry Deterding... the great inspiration and donor to anti-bolshevist campaigns were not denied."

Hitler received many millions of dollars from Deterding, Deterding's last residence was an estate in Germany, and a representative of the Hitler government spoke at his graveside.

There are numerous allusions and evidence in contemporary literature concerning Hitler's foreign financial sources, from which those previously quoted are but a few examples, and the following additional ones will be mentioned:

The Neue Zurcher Zeitung wrote in their daily edition of October 18, 1929, as the Nazi movement was beginning to grow to huge proportions, under the title "Non olet!" (Money doesn't smell!):

The unusual amount of propaganda released today by the National Socialists all over Germany, their costumes and soldier-games, all items costing large sums of money, demand the question: where is the money coming from? It can't possibly originate just from the organization itself, considering how the whole structure is put together. Where is it coming from? The Badische Beobachter, leading organ of central Baden... has very interesting information about financial sources flowing into the Hitler movement. They form a conclusion as to where the money for the extensive, costly apparatus of National Socialist agitation originates...Noteworthy for these inheritors of patriotism, who make daily accusations of treason against their opponents, and who estimate themselves especially highly for their absolute German-ness, is that the money behind their movement is mainly procured from abroad, A Dr. Gausser dealt with Swiss donors, the Munich art dealer Hanffstangel with the Americans, an engineer Jung and Dr. Krebs with Czechoslovakians, the university Professor Freiherr von Bissing collected money for the Hitler movement in Holland. The correspondence was treated with great care and took place only under disguised addresses. The name Hitler was never mentioned. He was always called "Wolfi" in the letters... money came also from Ford and large sums were given by big industrialists in Czechoslovakia — Along with the foreign source of the money goes, according to this report, its capitalistic origin, a characteristic that still plays the most substantial role in the financing of the National Socialist Party today, in addition to everything else known or suspected of the movement.

Finally the fact must be mentioned that on February 11, 1932 the Socialist delegate Paul Faure proved in the French Chambers that the Czech Skoda Works together with the European Industry and Finance Union, which works in connection with Schneider-Creuzot, paid out huge sums to Hitler's German National Socialist Party.

At the end of 1931 Hitler gave an explanation of foreign policy to the English— American press that fits perfectly with his opinions in the Warburg report. The Imprekoor of December 8, 1931 remarked under the title: "Hitler on His Knees Before World Finance."

The Nazis believe in the old illusion that they can rely upon England and America for support when faced with French imperialism. That is why in this speech Hitler assumed the English-American thesis of the "priority" of private over political debts. That is why he spiced up his explanations of the tribute question with several attacks on Paris, by speculating on growing anti-French sentiment especially in England...That is why he made an especially strong admission concerning the payment of English-American loans and credits.

The valuable testimony of Dodd will now be cited here. Dodd was the American ambassador in Berlin from 1933–1938. In this position he met many highly-placed American and German personalities. His notes were published by his children in 1943 as a book which became famous.

Hitler's support by American capital appears with unusual clarity in Dodd's diary. American bankers who were anxious about their investments in Germany supported Nazism without exception. After Hitler had come to power, American and English armament industries delivered war materials to him. Also rich Jews tolerated and assisted Hitler, among them the Warburgs. A few especially noteworthy remarks in Dodd's sketches are enough to illustrate the point.

Dodd writes of a rich New Yorker:

He was very strongly against the Russian Revolution and enthusiastic about Hitler's regime in Germany. He hates Jews and hopes to see them treated accordingly. Naturally he advised me to let Hitler go his own way. (p. 24)

Professor John Coar wished to speak with complete frank— ness. He told me that he had been a personal friend of Adolf Hitler's and in 1923 had advised him against his putsch in Bavaria. (So Hitler had American advisors among his circle already in 1923!) Hitler continued to give him interviews all the time and he was intending to go to Hitler's summer house in Bavaria in several days. He offered to bring me back an exact report of his conversation with Hitler, if I would give him a letter for President Roosevelt, to whom he wished to bring a final report. (p. 34)

Schacht is the real master here, and government

officials don't dare order him to do anything. (Entry of January 3,1934) (p. 82).

One evening my wife visited Baron Eberhard von Oppenheim, who lives splendidly and quietly near us. Many German Nazis were present. It is said that Oppenheim gave the Nazi party 200,000 marks, and that he had received a special party dispensation, declaring him to be an Aryan. (p. 86)

Ivy Lee and his son James came to lunch at 1:30. Ivy Lee proved to be both a capitalist and advocate of fascism at the same time. He told stories of his battle for the recognition of Russia, and was inclined to give credit for it. His sole endeavor was to raise American business profits, (p. 87)

Lazaron (an American rabbi) is here to gain information about possibilities for the Warburgs, who regret Rabbi Wise's extreme stand (against the Nazis), (p. 148)

The prominent Hamburg banker Max Warburg, brother of Felix Warburg in New York, came to the embassy to see me at the request of Rabbi Lazaron. The troubled life he had led in the last few years showed on him, and he was now in danger of losing his life if his views were ever made known to the government. He stayed one hour. He thinks Rabbi Wise and Samuel Untermyer in New York have severely jeopardized Jews living in the United-States as well as in Germany with their public outcry. He said Felix Warburg was of the same opinion. These two men are in complete agreement with Colonel House, who tries to ease the Jewish boycott (against Nazi Germany) and to reduce the number of Jews in high places in the United States. (p. 155)

I visited Eric Phipps and repeated confidentially a report that Armstrong-Vickers, the huge British armaments concern, had negotiated the sale of war materials here last week...Last Friday I told Sir Eric that British armament people were selling massive amounts of war materials here. I was frank enough — or indiscreet enough — to add that I understood representatives of Curtiss-Wright, from the U.S. were here to negotiate similar sales. (p. 186)

I told Lewis that Hearst has supported and visited Mussolini for five or six years. I informed him of Hearst's visit to Berlin last September and his deal with Goebbels that the German Propaganda Ministry should have all European Hearst-newspapers at the same time as the United States, (p. 221)

Poor Lazaron was very upset because so many rich Jews have capitulated to the Nazi leadership and are influential financial aides to Dr. Schaft, who finds their support in the present situation very important, (p. 236)

Even the Nuremberg Trials could not suppress the evidence of the once close, friendly and good relations between English-American capital, its governments and Hitler, in spite of the efforts of the court to guard zealously that this side of the issue was never raised, by declaring statements about it "irrelevant and immaterial." Schacht in particular mentioned this critical subject.

When Schacht brought up again the relations of foreign powers to the National Socialist regime and the assistance they bestowed upon it, the court decided that this information had nothing to do with the issue, and was therefore inadmissible...Schacht had let representatives of foreign powers convince him they should support the National Socialist government in its infancy. The court refused to admit all these statements. (NZZ no. 758, May 2, 1946)

Funk wrote a report (on the financial aid Hitler received from capitalists) that shed light on the early history of the Third Reich in an interesting way. The role of the donors must be given great importance, because their gifts and the assistance they otherwise granted promoted Hitler's rise extraordinarily. For that reason a heavy historical burden rests on the bankers and industrialists concerned. Along with Schacht, von Papen and Hugenberg they belong to the "steps of the ladder," that group of influential men who made important contributions to the final success of National Socialism. (NZZ no. 805, May 8, 1946)

Baldur von Schitach spoke more than an hour long about his youth and said, among other things, that it had been Henry Ford's book The International Jew that had converted him to anti-Semitism. (NZZ no. 916, May 24, 1946)

These are several illustrations of Hitler's support through foreign capitalists. This collection could go on forever. The examples mentioned are enough for our purposes.

Hitler was made not only by German capital, but primarily by international and especially America capital that intervened decisively from the beginning, from ca. 1920, in the battle for power in Germany. If this German battle for power had been decided within the Weimar Republic by German means only, then Hitler would never have won. Hitler became the strongest man in Germany because he had access to the strongest international assistance. His strength and success can only be understood at all when this fact is taken into account.

The Warburg report can be genuine. We do not assume that is genuine because we lack absolute proof (incidentally proof is also lacking to assume forgery). So the Warburg report remains a problem for the time being. One can certainly assume that the Warburg report is symbolically true, since it describes in a simple, generally understood and plain way the actual relations Hitler and American and international capital, evidence which has been proven a thousand times over. Hitler used American and international capital to cause World War II, to destroy and finally occupy Germany and Europe.

Who is worse, the instruments or their instigators, who subsequently wash their hands in innocence, and damn their own instruments and creations, disposing of them as dangerous witnesses in the end? An "order" that needs such instruments and means must be condemned.

The Warburg report, should it be genuine, is one of the most interesting and important documents of our epoch as it illuminates that whole area of darkness in which Hitler and the second World War were made, and because it proves that the core of international capital, American capital, is war criminal number one.

It is over and above a sociological and political "textbook" of the first order, because it presents relations between economy and politics of our time concretely, as living testimony, giving the reader a look into the secret inner chambers of the capitalist empire. At the same time it is a shattering document, because it is made abundantly clear that the unbelievable suffering and sacrifice of humanity in the last fifteen years were brought about and suffered in the interests of international and especially American high finance. It is an obligation to general power and to humanity to discover the truth about this report and to publicize and circulate it to this purpose.

October 1946.

Other titles

OMNIA VERITAS
Liberalism, more popularly known as secular humanism, can be traced in an unbroken line all the way back to the Biblical "Curse of Canaan."
Omnia Veritas Ltd presents:
THE CURSE OF CANAAN
A demonology of history
by
EUSTACE MULLINS
Humanism is the logical result of the demonology of history

OMNIA VERITAS
The peoples of the world not only will never love Big Brother, but they will soon dispose of him forever.
Omnia Veritas Ltd presents:
THE WORLD ORDER
OUR SECRET RULERS
A Study in the Hegemony of Parasitism
by
EUSTACE MULLINS
The program of the World Order remains the same; Divide and Conquer

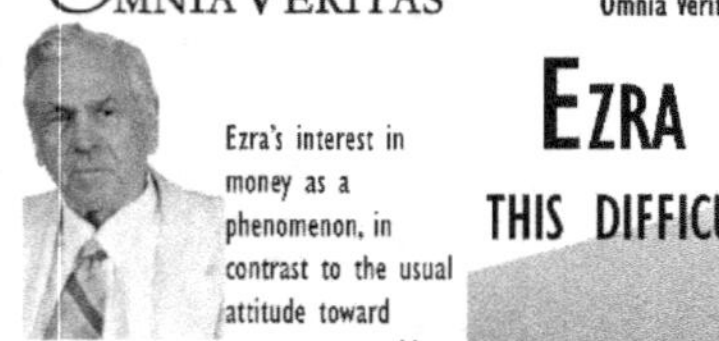
OMNIA VERITAS
Ezra's interest in money as a phenomenon, in contrast to the usual attitude toward money as something to get, is a legitimate one.
Omnia Veritas Ltd presents:
EZRA POUND
THIS DIFFICULT INDIVIDUAL
by
EUSTACE MULLINS
An illustration for his own monetary theories...

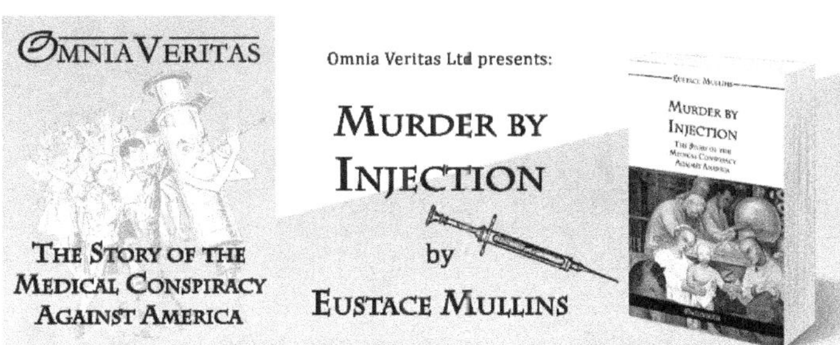
OMNIA VERITAS
THE STORY OF THE MEDICAL CONSPIRACY AGAINST AMERICA
Omnia Veritas Ltd presents:
MURDER BY INJECTION
by
EUSTACE MULLINS
MURDER BY INJECTION
THE STORY OF THE MEDICAL CONSPIRACY AGAINST AMERICA
The cynicism and malice of these conspirators is something beyond the imagination of most Americans.

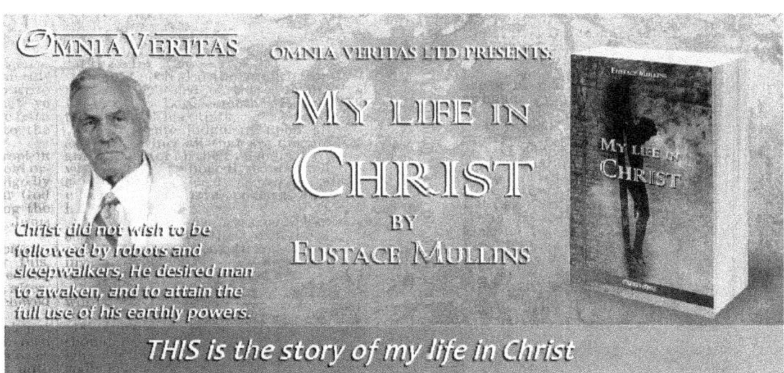
OMNIA VERITAS
Christ did not wish to be followed by robots and sleepwalkers, He desired man to awaken, and to attain the full use of his earthly powers.
OMNIA VERITAS LTD PRESENTS:
MY LIFE IN CHRIST
BY
EUSTACE MULLINS
MY LIFE IN CHRIST
THIS is the story of my life in Christ

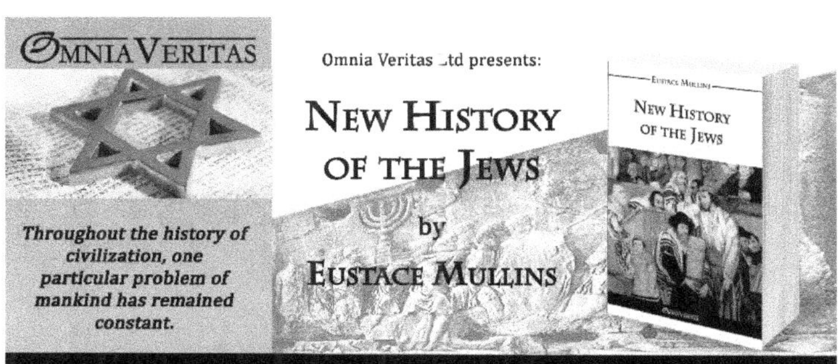
OMNIA VERITAS
Throughout the history of civilization, one particular problem of mankind has remained constant.
Omnia Veritas Ltd presents:
NEW HISTORY OF THE JEWS
by
EUSTACE MULLINS
NEW HISTORY OF THE JEWS
Only one people has irritated its host nations in every part of the civilized world

OMNIA VERITAS
AMERICA'S TRIBUNALS
EXPOSED
SPIRIT OF JUSTICE

EUSTACE MULLINS
THE RAPE OF
JUSTICE
AMERICA'S TRIBUNALS EXPOSED

OMNIA VERITAS
UNITED STATES
FEDERAL RESERVE SYSTEM
HERE ARE THE SIMPLE
FACTS OF THE GREAT
BETRAYAL

EUSTACE MULLINS
THE SECRETS OF THE
FEDERAL RESERVE
THE LONDON CONNECTION

OMNIA VERITAS
The hidden origin of
Whahhabism finally revealed!

Confessions
of a
British Spy

OMNIA VERITAS
... it appears to me that the world is very much as it was-that Eden is still possible to those who are fit for it...
Omnia Veritas Ltd presents:
Courtship and Marriage and The Gentle Art of Home-Making
BY ANNIE S. SWAN
Courtship And Marriage And The Gentle Art Of Home-Making
Every man goes to woo in his own way...

OMNIA VERITAS
Discover the Secret behind the Muslim Brotherhood, the globalist's tool for world dominion.
Omnia Veritas Ltd presents :
THE Globalists & Islamists
Fomenting the "Clash of Civilizations" for a New World Order
THE Globalists & Islamists
Who is pulling the string of Radical Islam ?
You will find out reading this astonishing work of Peter Goodgame!

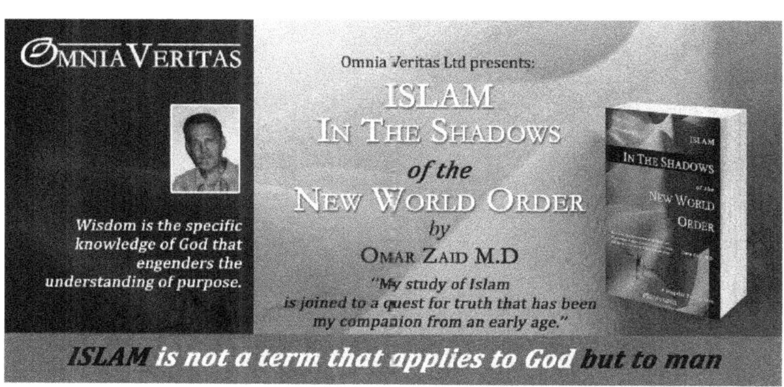

OMNIA VERITAS
Wisdom is the specific knowledge of God that engenders the understanding of purpose.
Omnia Veritas Ltd presents:
ISLAM IN THE SHADOWS of the NEW WORLD ORDER
by
OMAR ZAID M.D
"My study of Islam is joined to a quest for truth that has been my companion from an early age."
ISLAM
IN THE SHADOWS
of the
NEW WORLD
ORDER
ISLAM is not a term that applies to God but to man

OMNIA VERITAS
The meaning
of Monarchy's
struggle against
the Money Power
Omnia Veritas Ltd presents:
Monarchy
or
Money
POWER
by
ROBERT McNAIR WILSON
A master-piece of history
The true nature of Kingship revealed!

OMNIA VERITAS
Omnia Veritas Ltd presents:
NUREMBERG
OR THE PROMISED LAND
by MAURICE BARDÈCHE
I am not taking up the
defense of Germany. I am
taking up the defense of
the truth.
MAURICE BARDÈCHE
NUREMBERG
OR THE PROMISED LAND
We have lived with a falsification of history

OMNIA VERITAS
A classic work
that exposes the
fraudulent nature
of the banking
system and the huge
and detrimental
impact it has on all
our lives.
Omnia Veritas Ltd presents:
PROMISE
to
PAY
by
ROBERT McNAIR WILSON
An inquiry into
The Modern Magic
called
"HIGH FINANCE"
PROMISE
to
PAY
The creation of money should be in the hands of the State or Head of Government
and not in the hands of private banking.

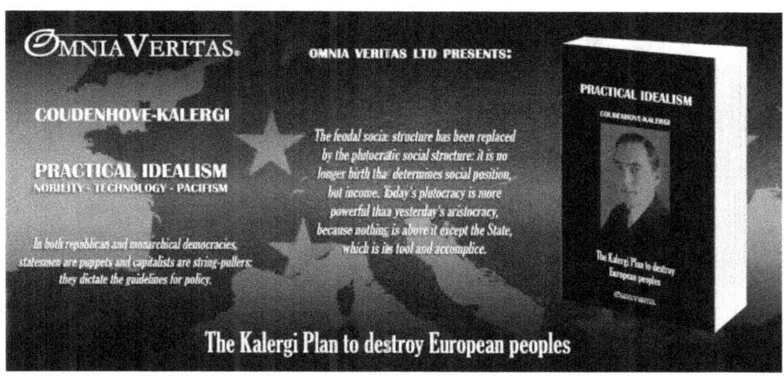
OMNIA VERITAS
OMNIA VERITAS LTD PRESENTS:
COUDENHOVE-KALERGI
PRACTICAL IDEALISM
NOBILITY - TECHNOLOGY - PACIFISM
In both republican and monarchical democracies, statesmen are puppets and capitalists are string-pullers: they dictate the guidelines for policy.
The feudal social structure has been replaced by the plutocratic social structure: it is no longer birth that determines social position, but income. Today's plutocracy is more powerful than yesterday's aristocracy, because nothing is above it except the State, which is its tool and accomplice.
PRACTICAL IDEALISM
COUDENHOVE-KALERGI
The Kalergi Plan to destroy European peoples
The Kalergi Plan to destroy European peoples

OMNIA VERITAS
UNDERSTAND ILLUMINATI CULT PROGRAMMING

Omnia Veritas Ltd presents:
SVALI SPEAKS
BREAKING FREE OF CULT PROGRAMMING
SVALI SPEAKS
BREAKING FREE OF CULT PROGRAMMING
Modern day Illuminism is a philosophy funded by the wealthy

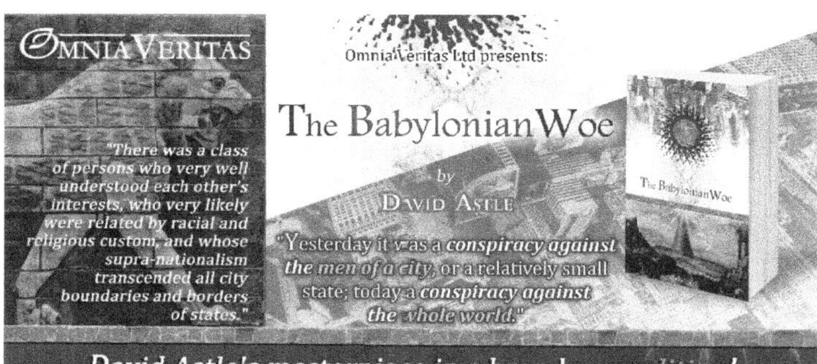
OMNIA VERITAS
"There was a class of persons who very well understood each other's interests, who very likely were related by racial and religious custom, and whose supra-nationalism transcended all city boundaries and borders of states."
Omnia Veritas Ltd presents:
The Babylonian Woe
by
DAVID ASTLE
"Yesterday it was a conspiracy against the men of a city, or a relatively small state; today a conspiracy against the whole world."
The Babylonian Woe
David Astle's masterpiece in a brand new edition!

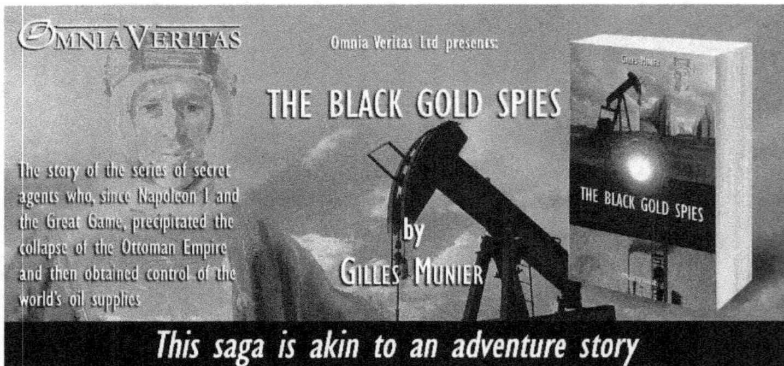
OMNIA VERITAS
Omnia Veritas Ltd presents:
THE BLACK GOLD SPIES
The story of the series of secret agents who, since Napoleon I and the Great Game, precipitated the collapse of the Ottoman Empire and then obtained control of the world's oil supplies
by
GILLES MUNIER
THE BLACK GOLD SPIES
This saga is akin to an adventure story

OMNIA VERITAS
Omnia Veritas Ltd presents :
THE CONTROVERSY OF ZION
by
Douglas Reed
Douglas Reed's book is the missing link unveiling the multisecular plot.
Zionism:
Centuries of Struggle to reclaim the Holy Land
THE CONTROVERSY OF ZION
Resurrected true history !

OMNIA VERITAS
Historians are finding less and less to celebrate about the Revolution...
Omnia Veritas Ltd presents:
THE FRENCH Revolution
A Study in Democracy
by
NESTA WEBSTER
An account of the bloody terror, the mob violence, and the overthrow of French religious tradition...
Hard political and historical facts compiled in this essential classic!

Omnia Veritas Ltd presents:

The Gentlemen's Book of Etiquette, and Manual of Politeness

A complete guide for a gentleman's conduct in all his relations towards society

BY

CECIL B. HARTLEY

To make your **politeness** part of yourself, inseparable from every action, is the height of **gentlemanly** elegance and finish of **manner**.

As you treat the world, so the world will treat you

Omnia Veritas Ltd presents:

The Ladies' Book of Etiquette, and Manual of Politeness

A complete hand book for the use of the lady in polite society

BY

FLORENCE HARTLEY

... to be truly a **lady**, one must carry the **principles** into every circumstance of life

Politeness is goodness of heart put into daily practice

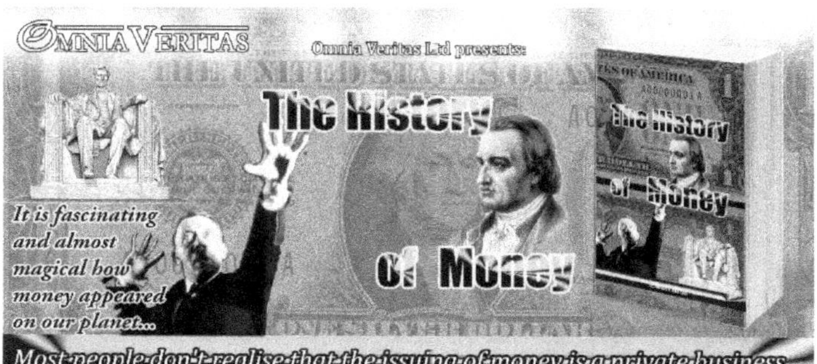

OMNIA VERITAS
Omnia Veritas Ltd presents:
THE HIGH COST OF VENGEANCE
THE HIGH COST OF VENGEANCE
France and Britain refused to listen to the statesmen who said that you can have peace or vengeance, not both...
BY FREDA UTLEY
The victors refused even to discuss the terms of peace with the vanquished

OMNIA VERITAS
Omnia Veritas Ltd presents:
A free press is the guardian genius of a just, honest, and humane democracy, as Lincoln put it:
"To sin by silence when they know they should protest, makes cowards of men."
THE LEGALIZED CRIME OF BANKING
THE LEGALIZED CRIME OF BANKING
by
SILAS WALTER ADAMS
"There is a great deal of difference between a moral wrong and a legal right"
A liberating and much acclaimed book on the Federal Reserve system!

OMNIA VERITAS
Omnia Veritas Ltd presents:
ARCHIBALD RAMSAY
THE NAMELESS WAR
ARCHIBALD RAMSAY
THE NAMELESS WAR
THE JEWISH POWER AGAINST THE NATIONS
The author describes the anatomy of the machine of the Revolutionary International which today pursues the project of supranational world power, the age-old messianic dream of international Jewry...
THE JEWISH POWER AGAINST THE NATIONS
Evidence of a centuries-old conspiracy against Europe and the whole of Christendom...

OMNIA VERITAS
It can be stated without fear of exaggeration that no book in the present century has been the object of so many commentaries in the world press...

MAURICE PINAY
The plot against the Church

OMNIA VERITAS

the Jews, however, in spite of their dispersion amongst the nations...

THE RIDDLE OF THE JEW'S SUCCESS

OMNIA VERITAS
"If we do not restore the Institution of Property we cannot escape restoring the Institution of Slavery; there is no third course."

OMNIA VERITAS

The **moral** nature of an act does not depend on the enacted statutes of human **legislators**, and the laws of economics are **eternal**.

Omnia Veritas Ltd presents:

USURY,
A Scriptural, Ethical and Economic View

BY CALVIN ELLIOT

The word usury was very odious to the Christian mind and conscience

OMNIA VERITAS

To understand the world we live in, we must understand the symbols surrounding us.

Omnia Veritas Ltd presents :

The VigilantCitizen
"Symbols Rule The World, Not Words Nor Laws"

ARTICLES COMPILATION

The occult symbolism
in movies & music

The occult references of the entertainment industry !

OMNIA VERITAS

Yes, **love** is a **woman's** whole life. Some **modern women** might object to this...

Omnia Veritas Ltd presents:

Woman,
her Sex and
Love Life

by WILLIAM J. ROBINSON M.D.

they will tell you if you enjoy their confidence that they are unhappy...

OMNIA VERITAS
Omnia Veritas Ltd presents:
MYRON FAGAN
THE ILLUMINATI
AND THE
COUNCIL ON FOREIGN RELATIONS
The objective is to brainwash the people into accepting the phony peace bait to transform the United States into an enslaved unit of the United Nations' one-world government.
They have seized that power on orders from their masters of the great conspiracy

OMNIA VERITAS
OMNIA VERITAS LTD PRESENTS
THE DISPOSSESSED MAJORITY
THE DISPOSSESSED MAJORITY
THE TRAGIC AND HUMILIATING FATE OF THE AMERICAN MAJORITY

OMNIA VERITAS
Omnia Veritas Ltd presents:
FREDERICK SODDY
THE ROLE OF MONEY
WHAT IT SHOULD BE CONTRASTED WITH WHAT IT HAS BECOME
FREDERICK SODDY
THE ROLE OF MONEY
This book attempts to clear up the mystery of money in its social aspect
This, surely, is what the public really wants to know about money

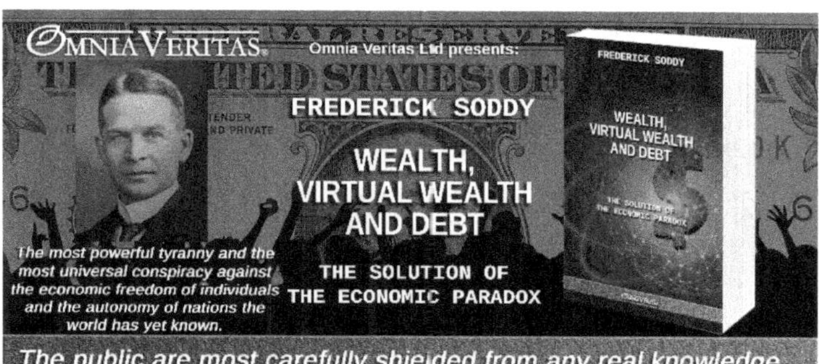
OMNIA VERITAS
Omnia Veritas Ltd presents:
FREDERICK SODDY
WEALTH, VIRTUAL WEALTH AND DEBT
THE SOLUTION OF THE ECONOMIC PARADOX
The most powerful tyranny and the most universal conspiracy against the economic freedom of individuals and the autonomy of nations the world has yet known.
The public are most carefully shielded from any real knowledge...
FREDERICK SODDY
WEALTH, VIRTUAL WEALTH AND DEBT
THE SOLUTION OF THE ECONOMIC PARADOX

OMNIA VERITAS
Omnia Veritas Ltd presents:
HERVÉ RYSSEN
History of anti-Semitism
set straight by a goy
The history of Judaism is the history of a people - or a sect - at permanent war against the rest of humanity...
After reading this book, we hope that no one will speak of "Judeo-Christian" civilisation any more...
HERVÉ RYSSEN
History of anti-Semitism
set straight by a goy

OMNIA VERITAS
Omnia Veritas Ltd presents:
HERVÉ RYSSEN
ISRAEL'S BILLIONS
Since time immemorial, spread in all countries, they are famous for having dedicated themselves to the great international trade. They are also, for centuries, the masters of banking and speculation.
Jews have a very particular relationship with money...
HERVÉ RYSSEN
ISRAEL'S BILLIONS

OMNIA VERITAS
Omnia Veritas Ltd presents:
HERVÉ RYSSEN
PLANETARIAN HOPES
The triumph of democracy over communism seemed to have opened the door to a new era, to a "New World Order", and to prepare all nations for an inevitable planetary merger.
HERVÉ RYSSEN
PLANETARIAN HOPES
The idea of a world without borders and of a finally unified humanity is certainly not new...

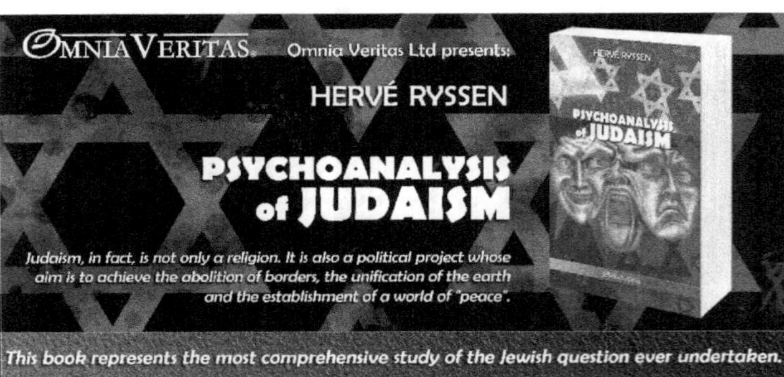
OMNIA VERITAS
Omnia Veritas Ltd presents:
HERVÉ RYSSEN
PSYCHOANALYSIS of JUDAISM
Judaism, in fact, is not only a religion. It is also a political project whose aim is to achieve the abolition of borders, the unification of the earth and the establishment of a world of "peace".
HERVÉ RYSSEN
PSYCHOANALYSIS of JUDAISM
This book represents the most comprehensive study of the Jewish question ever undertaken.

OMNIA VERITAS
Omnia Veritas Ltd presents:
HERVÉ RYSSEN
THE JEWISH FANATICISM
The resulting dissolution of national identity protects them from a possible nationalist backlash against the power they gained, especially in finance, politics and the media.
HERVÉ RYSSEN
THE JEWISH FANATICISM
The Jewish people promote a project for the whole of humanity...

OMNIAVERITAS
Omnia Veritas Ltd presents:
HERVÉ RYSSEN
The Jewish mafia is, however, undoubtedly the most powerful mafia in the world. The most dangerous, too. Some overly curious journalists have already been killed.
The Jewish Mafia
HERVE RYSSEN
The Jewish Mafia
International Predators
The "Jewish mafia", that one, does not exist; the Western media do not talk about it...

OMNIAVERITAS
MK ULTRA
Ritual Abuse and Mind Control
Tools of domination for the nameless religion
For the first time, a book attempts to explore the complex subjects of traumatic ritual abuse and the mind control that results from it...
ALEXANDRE LEBRETON
MK ULTRA
Ritual Abuse and Mind Control
Tools of domination for the nameless religion
How is it possible to mentally program a human being?

OMNIAVERITAS
Omnia Veritas Ltd presents:
THE SVALI CHRONICLES
BREAKING FREE FROM MIND CONTROL
TESTIMONY OF AN EX-ILLUMINATI
The Illuminati are a group of people who follow a philosophy known as "Illuminism" or "enlightenment".
THE SVALI CHRONICLES
Understanding the programming of the Illuminati sect

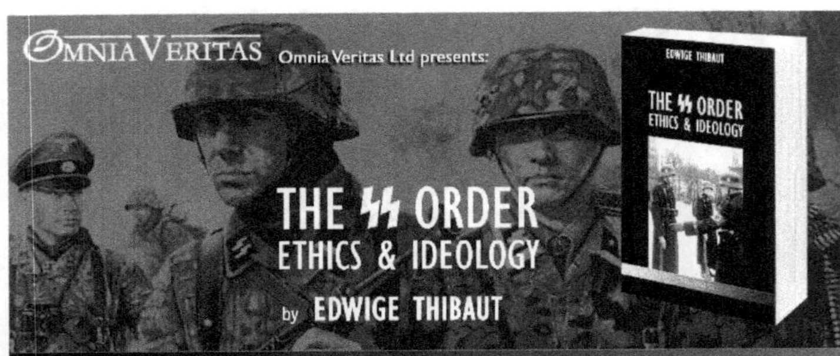
OMNIA VERITAS
OmniaVeritas Ltd presents:
EDWIGE THIBAUT
THE SS ORDER
ETHICS & IDEOLOGY
THE SS ORDER
ETHICS & IDEOLOGY
by EDWIGE THIBAUT
The most extraordinary political-military formation that humanity has ever known

OMNIA VERITAS
OMNIA VERITAS LTD PRESENTS:
JOHN COLEMAN
ABORTION
GENOCIDE IN AMERICA
BY JOHN COLEMAN
ABORTION
GENOCIDE IN AMERICA
I MAINTAIN THAT WHEN A WOMAN AGREES TO
AN ABORTION IN A NON-LIFE THREATENING
SITUATION, SHE HAS TAKEN LEAVE OF HER
SENSES AND SHOULD BE ADJUDGED
"TEMPORARILY INSANE."
ABORTION SHOULD BE EXPLAINED AS EUPHEMISM FOR "MURDER BY DECEPTION"

OMNIA VERITAS
OMNIA VERITAS LTD PRESENTS:
JOHN COLEMAN
BEYOND the
CONSPIRACY
UNMASKING THE INVISIBLE
WORLD GOVERNMENT
BEYOND the
CONSPIRACY
All great historical events are
planned in secret by men who
surround themselves with total
discretion.
by John Coleman
Highly organized groups always have the advantage over citizens

OMNIA VERITAS
OMNIA VERITAS LTD PRESENTS:
THE CLUB OF ROME
THE THINK TANK OF THE NEW WORLD ORDER
BY JOHN COLEMAN
The many tragic and explosive events of the 20th century didn't happen by themselves, but were planned according to a well-established pattern...
Who were the planners and creators of these major events?
JOHN COLEMAN
THE CLUB OF ROME

OMNIA VERITAS
OMNIA VERITAS LTD PRESENTS:
DIPLOMACY BY DECEPTION
AN ACCOUNT OF THE TREASONOUS CONDUCT
BY THE GOVERNMENTS OF BRITAIN AND THE UNITED STATES
BY
JOHN COLEMAN
The story of the creation of the United Nations is a classic case of diplomacy by deception
JOHN COLEMAN
DIPLOMACY BY DECEPTION

OMNIA VERITAS
OMNIA VERITAS LTD PRESENTS:
DRUG WAR against AMERICA
BY JOHN COLEMAN
The drug trade cannot be eradicated because its directors will not allow the world's most lucrative market to be taken away from them...
The real promoters of this cursed trade are the "elites" of this world.
JOHN COLEMAN
DRUG WAR against AMERICA

OMNIA VERITAS
OMNIA VERITAS LTD PRESENTS:
FREEMASONRY
from A to Z
by John Coleman
In the 21st century, Freemasonry has become less a secret society than a "society of secrets".
This book explains what masonry is
JOHN COLEMAN
FREEMASONRY
from A to Z

OMNIA VERITAS
OMNIA VERITAS LTD PRESENTS:
THE ROTHSCHILD DYNASTY
by John Coleman
Historical events are often caused by a "hidden hand"...
JOHN COLEMAN
THE ROTHSCHILD DYNASTY

OMNIA VERITAS
OMNIA VERITAS LTD PRESENTS:
ONE WORLD ORDER
SOCIALIST DICTATORSHIP
All these years, while our attention was focused on the evils of communism in Moscow, the socialists in Washington were busy stealing from America!
BY JOHN COLEMAN
"The enemy in Washington is more to be feared than the enemy in Moscow."
JOHN COLEMAN
ONE WORLD ORDER SOCIALIST DICTATORSHIP

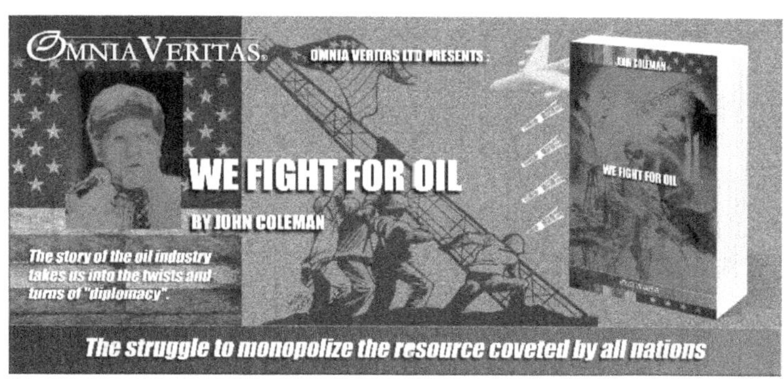
OMNIA VERITAS.
OMNIA VERITAS LTD PRESENTS :
WE FIGHT FOR OIL
BY JOHN COLEMAN
The story of the oil industry takes us into the twists and turns of "diplomacy".
JOHN COLEMAN
WE FIGHT FOR OIL
The struggle to monopolize the resource coveted by all nations

OMNIA VERITAS.
LIGHT-BEARERS OF DARKNESS
This book is an attempt to show, by means of documentary evidence, that the actual world conditions are under the influence of mystic and secret societies through which the Invisible Centre is seeking to direct and dominate the nations and the world.
LIGHT-BEARERS OF DARKNESS

OMNIA VERITAS.
THE TRAIL OF THE SERPENT
An attempt to trace the worship of the ancient Serpent, the Creative Principle, the God of all initiates of the Gnostics and Cabalists, emanating from the Hellenised Jews of Alexandria.
THE TRAIL OF THE SERPENT

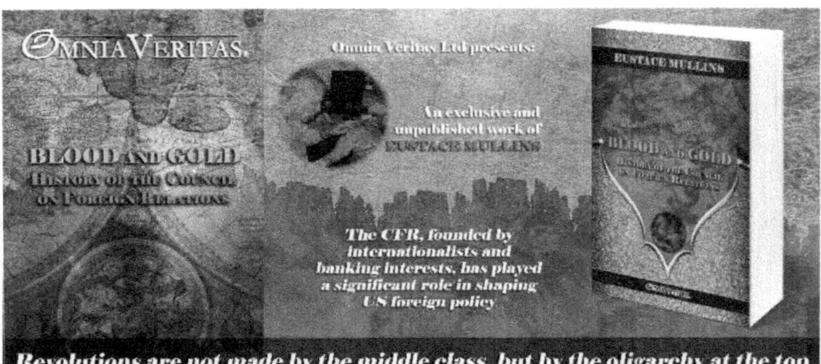
OMNIA VERITAS.
Omnia Veritas Ltd presents:
An exclusive and unpublished work of EUSTACE MULLINS
BLOOD AND GOLD
HISTORY OF THE COUNCIL ON FOREIGN RELATIONS
The CFR, founded by internationalists and banking interests, has played a significant role in shaping US foreign policy
EUSTACE MULLINS
BLOOD AND GOLD
Revolutions are not made by the middle class, but by the oligarchy at the top

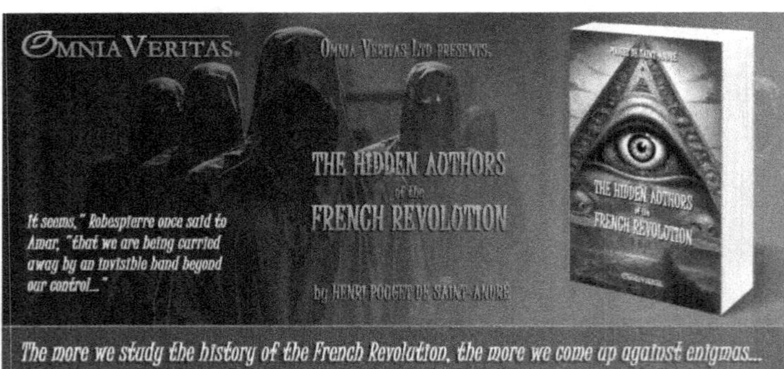
OMNIA VERITAS.
OMNIA VERITAS LTD PRESENTS,
THE HIDDEN AUTHORS of the FRENCH REVOLUTION
It seems," Robespierre once said to Amar, "that we are being carried away by an invisible hand beyond our control..."
by HENRI POGGET DE SAINT-ANDRÉ
THE HIDDEN AUTHORS of the FRENCH REVOLUTION
The more we study the history of the French Revolution, the more we come up against enigmas...

OMNIA VERITAS®
www.omnia-veritas.com

www.ingramcontent.com/pod-product-compliance
Lightning Source LLC
Chambersburg PA
CBHW060930050726

47592CB00003B/886